Until You Cry

Luna Dolmen

Copyright © 2024 by Luna Dolmen

All rights reserved.

No portion of this book may be reproduced in any form without written permission from the publisher or author, except as permitted by U.S. copyright law.

Contents

1 Beginnings	1
2 Movie Nights	13
3 Monday Mopes	23
4 Party Planning	34
5 Birthday Parties	42
6 Fighting	55
7 Broken Hearts	65
8 Tennessee	79
9 Thanksgiving-1	94
10 Thanksgiving- 2	116
11 Panicking	129
12 More Trouble	136
13 Avoiding Him	147
14 Talking	161
15 Coffee	169

16 Holiday Plans	177
17 Second Guessing	188
18 Mixed Emotions	197
19 Discussions	208
20 Shopping	223
21 Christmas Time	232
22 New Year	240
23 Back To School	251
24 Epilogues	260

1 Beginnings

Relationships are hard. It's common knowledge. In most of the books and the movies, they look easy most of the time but that's because they usually only cover the Cupcake Phase. You know, that part of the relationship right after two people get together and they're just absolutely in love with each other. Everything that the other person does is adorable and cute. However, after a while, the Cupcake Phase wears off and both people are hit with a cold dose of reality and it absolutely stinks. My theory is that the cute couples aren't the ones that look cute during the Cupcake Phase because let's face it, every couple looks cute during this time period. The really cute couples are the couples that make it through the Cupcake Phase. Together and alive. The transition is really hard though.

The way she speaks along to the lines in a movie that she knows goes from adorable to irritating.

The way he gets jealous when other guys look at her goes from chivalry to suffocating.

Everything that somebody does goes from absolutely cute to incredibly annoying.

So this is the story about what happens after the Cupcake Phase. After the two people meet (I met Andrew freshman year) and after they get together (He asked me out almost five months ago) and after the rose-colored Cupcake Phase (That ended about a month ago). After the first date, the first kiss, the first 'I love you'. What the movies don't tell you.

"Can we go do something?" I ask my boyfriend of five months, Andrew, as he's sitting in his dorm room, aggressively pushing the buttons on his video game controller.

"In a little bit, Babe," He assures me in a distracted mumble as he continues to glare at the TV screen in complete concentration. "I just have to finish this game and then I'll turn it off."

I roll my eyes and sit down on the bed beside him so that I'm not just awkwardly standing around doing nothing. "There's always another game to finish. Can't you just pause it for a little bit?"

"It's a live game," He insists as if I should already know that. Video games aren't really my thing though and, no matter how hard he tries, I will not understand what that means or why that means he can't pause the stupid game. "I can't pause it or I forfeit, which I can't do. I'll be done in about an hour though."

"Our curfew is in forty-five minutes," I remind him dryly. Both of us go to the Vaughn Dance Academy which is a boarding school for high school students who have a strong interest in dance. The Vaughn Schools are incredibly prestigious and known globally for the impressive talent that they produce so basically, we're the best of the best dancers in our age group from America. We live in dorms just like all boarding schools and we have a curfew at ten o'clock during the school week, which is when the dorm buildings lock up for the night. Nobody can get in or out, so it's pretty important that I'm back at my own dorm by that time. If you get locked out, you have to go to the security guard who will let you into your room and also write you up with a week of detention for being out after curfew. I mean, Andrew and I live in the same dorm building but we're on different floors. That's the rules of the school, the boys and girls have to live on separate floors, and not only do the outside doors lock but the elevators lock too. They don't lock the doors to the stairs because of safety hazards but they have well-watched cameras on the stairwells. Most of the time, the school gives us a lot of freedom, but they are very strict when it comes to school night curfew.

"Oh," Andrew mumbles absentmindedly. He's obviously paying more attention to his stupid game than he is to me which has become a habit of his lately. I used to think that his passion for these games was cute but now he's pretty much ignoring me almost all of the time and it's not so cute anymore. "Well, we can hang out tomorrow then."

"I can't tomorrow," I sigh in annoyance. "I have my chiropractor thing tomorrow." Because being a dancer puts a lot of stress on the body, so I have to go see a chiropractor at least once a month to make sure that everything is in place and working well. That's one of the requirements for going to this school and some people go more than once a month but once a month is the minimum during the school year.

"Stella, you act like we never see each other," He laughs but I honestly don't find anything funny about that. "We see each other every day."

"We haven't hung out in over a week," I mutter. "You've been glued to your TV for days now. I mean, we see each other in class but we never really talk anymore, you're always playing this game."

"It's a tournament thing though, I have to," Andrew tells me, biting his bottom lip in concentration which is another thing that I used to think was so cute, the way he bites his lip when he's concentrating on his game. "It'll be over soon though, in just a few days."

"Yeah, whatever," I try to show him how unhappy I am with how he's just kind of ignoring me but I don't think he hears my distaste because he's so focused on his game. He's not paying any attention to me and it's not like I'm an attention whore or anything, I just think I'd be nice for my boyfriend to actually notice me sometimes is all. "I'm leaving. I'll see you tomorrow?"

He doesn't even nod or anything, he just says, "Uh, yeah. Tomorrow."

I run my fingers through his short blonde hair and then kiss his cheek because I don't want to leave on a completely horrid note. I want him to remember that I'm still his girlfriend and even though he's kind of putting me on the backburner, I'm still here. I'm still his girlfriend. "I love you."

"I love you too, Stella," He informs me but he doesn't sound too sincere. It's not because he doesn't love me though, because I know that he does, it's just his distraction with the video game. He tried to teach it to me a while ago but I never understood the stupid game. I never call the game stupid in front of him though because he doesn't like that, but I think it's stupid. It's complicated and violent and I don't understand it at all.

I leave the room, shutting the door behind me and walking into the hallway. Our dorm building is only for the seniors at Vaughn because the seniors get special dorms. As opposed to the other dorm buildings for the lower classmen that have two beds per room, the seniors don't have to share a room with a roommate, we get individual rooms and therefor, more space. We also have our own bathrooms in our dorms but the underclassmen have to share the community bathrooms with stalls and stuff like that. So I go to the stairs and trot up the stairs just one flight because my dorm room is just one level on top of Andrew's and walk into my room. It has an intense smell of expensive perfume and makeup that Andrew hates but he used to think it was cute how I had a science to the way I smelled each day. He liked the way that I smelled but now he cringes whenever he walks into my room because of the flowery smell.

Getting dressed in my pajamas that consist of short shorts and one of Andrew's shirts, I decide that tonight is going to be an early night for me. Usually if I'm not with Andrew, I'm with one or both of my two best friends but they're both out with their own boyfriends right now and I don't want to interrupt their nice night. They have boyfriends that don't value video games more than them. It must be nice. I mean, I'm not one of those girls that give their boyfriends ultimatums. I never told him that it's either the video games or it's me. I never tried to get him to quit playing video games, I just think that it'd be nice if he didn't play them all of the time.

I sit down on my comfortable twin sized bed and turn on my TV to try and find something on TV and finally land on Keeping Up With the Kardashians before I grab a few slices of salami from my mini fridge and then snuggle up in my soft blankets and listen to all of the wise words of the Kardashians.

Ashton said the monkey had pooped on him, so I didn't feel too bad. Gross little monkey!

Me too, Kim. Me too.

~~~~

The next morning is a Friday so I have to get up at four in the morning for a half an hour jog around campus and then have enough time to shower and change before I have to get to class. Because I go to a dance school, our schedules are a little different than traditional schools which is to be expected.

We have eight periods, which is pretty average, but the way that they're divided is a little different. We have four periods of academic courses, a lunch, a dance ethics course, and then a two-period studio dance class that changes each semester. The dance ethics course is a class that's taught in a classroom like a normal class but it's about dance. For example, The History of European Dance or Hispanic Dance Culture.

I grab breakfast with my two best friends, Sienna and Mason, in the food court half an hour before our first class starts which is what we always do. I have first period Calculus with Sienna but Mason has physics. All of the academic classes are in the same building though, so we're all headed to the same place after breakfast.

"What's got you in the dumps today?" Mason asks me as she's eating her nutritious breakfast of a muffin and some fruit. It almost mirrors my own breakfast except I don't have pineapple in my fruit because I'm pretty allergic. I like to watch what I eat though, because all of my working out would be for nothing if I just filled up on calories all of the time.

"Yeah, you seem kinda off," Sienna agrees with Mason. Sienna's breakfast is completely different than mine and Mason's. She's obviously not afraid of the calories or she has a superhuman metabolism because she eats like a pregnant cow but I have known her for seven months and she has never gained a pound. However, her breakfast plate is a mountain of pancakes, bacon, eggs, syrup, and hash browns. She defies science.

"Just Andrew being Andrew," I shrug. "I mean, it's totally unfair. Your boyfriend goes to college like, fifteen minutes away and you still see him more than I see Andrew, who only lives one freaking floor below me." Sienna met her boyfriend, Penn, over the summer and they seem to be surviving post-Cupcake very well. They see each other at least every weekend and most weeks, he'll drive over here and see her during the week too after classes and he'll take her out to dinner and stuff. He has a roommate in the dorms at UCLA (University of California- Los Angeles) so they have more privacy here since Sienna is a senior too and has her own dorm.

It's not much privacy considering how thin the walls are, but it's privacy nonetheless.

"He'll come around," Mason assures me. "Once he realizes that he's being a dick, he'll be apologizing with roses and fancy dates. Andrew can be really sweet when he wants to be."

I sigh a very long and very sad sigh because I don't think that Mason is right. Not about him being sweet, because that part is true, the part about him coming around though, it doesn't seem to be happening. Her boyfriend, Brian, is another one of my best friends and he's also a sweetheart. After being together for over half of a year, they have survived the post-Cupcake era pretty well just like Penn and Sienna (or as I like to call them, Pienna) did so well. Brian goes here too and he's a senior like us, so he stays in our building too so he and Mason are inseparable most of the time. Even after being together for so long, they still can't get enough of each other. Andrew and I have been together three months less than Mason and Brian and he's already getting sick of me. I try not to compare our relationship with my friends' but I can't help it. They are all so happy all of the time and it just doesn't seem like Andrew and I are as happy as we should be.

"It'll be okay. You two will work through it," Sienna supports Mason's theory.

"That's easy for you guys to say," I mumble, poking at my muffin some more. I'm not really all that hungry this morning so I'll probably just throw my food away and wait until lunch to eat. "You both have perfect boyfriends."

"You have a perfect boyfriend too, Stell," Sienna rolls her eyes at me. "You just have to work through the hard parts. I fight with Penn sometimes too, we just work through it."

"She's right," Mason adds. We have twenty minutes to get to class so we all get up from the table to leave for class and throw our trash away on our way out the door. "Relationships aren't always easy. You love Andrew and he loves you so you guys will figure it out, I know it. Sometimes it just takes some work to figure things out."

"I know," I sigh. "It just sucks, all of this fighting, I guess. Let's talk about something else though."

"Let's talk about the new girls then," Mason suggests. "The Ortega Twins."

"Oh yeah, Charlotte and Heather," Sienna adds. "I've heard about them but I haven't met either one of them yet."

"Me either," I pipe, grateful to be off of the topic of boys and onto the topic of gossip. Gossip is what I do best. The Ortega Twins have just arrived yesterday to this school which makes them the talk of the school right now. Because this school is so prestigious, it's really hard to transfer in if you don't start here during freshman year like everybody else. The rumors around the school have varied about how they got in. The first one is that they're both double threats (they can sing and dance) so they were going to the Vaughn School of Vocal Music but something happened to Heather's voice so they came here to dance instead because they're completely inseparable. The other big rumor is that they are transferring from some super awesome dance school in England. Either way, they're obviously really good dancers if they can squeeze their way into a school like this right in the middle of the year. "I hope they're nice at least."

"They're not," Mason sighs in confirmation. "The Charlotte one is a brat. I went into the office yesterday to get my mail and they were in there getting their schedules. She seems like a real know-it-all but I didn't hear Heather say anything. Anyway, I'd stay away from them."

I groan loudly as we all walk into the academic building with my friends along with a huge amount of other people that are on their way to their first period classes on this gloomy Friday morning. "We just got rid of Gianna. We do not need another one," I say, referring to Gianna Tarver who had been a major pain in the ass to me and all of my friends since freshman year. Well, except for Sienna because she only arrived at the school over the summer for the summer dance program that the school has and then she continued into the school for her senior year (she got in late because her uncle is the owner of the Vaughn schools so he pulled some strings and got her in easily). Anyway, Gianna made a mess of everything when we came here freshman year. She dated my twin brother for way too long and then broke his heart last summer (I didn't feel too bad because he was a dick anyway) and she was always trying to sabotage me and my friends because she was so insecure about her dancing but she also felt incredibly entitled because her mother was on the school board until recently. Anyway, Gianna and her goon, Ada Rivers, were expelled over the summer for trying to blow us up with firecrackers at the end of the summer so she doesn't go here anymore and it's magical. I finally know peace.

"Very true," Mason confirms with a nod. "I don't think she's as bad as Gianna though."

"I don't think anybody is as bad as Gianna," Sienna laughs.

We approach the busy hallway that splits into two different departments- math and science- which is where Mason has to say goodbye to go to physics down one hallway but Sienna and myself have to go the other way to make it to calculus.

"I guess we'll see how it goes. See you guys at lunch," Mason shrugs, waving us a quick goodbye before walking down the hallway towards her classroom.

"I'm sure these new twins aren't that bad," Sienna assures me, always being the voice of optimism. "I mean, if you dealt with Gianna and Ada for three years, I'm sure that these twins will seem like itty bitty flies to us now."

"You are so right," I laugh. "If we have to, we can take them but hopefully, Mason is wrong and they are actually lovely people."

We walk into our calculus room and sit down in our assigned seats which are in the middle of the room. We got to choose our seats at the beginning of the year, so we sit next to each other, but we have to keep those same seats for the rest of the year and if you're not in your assigned seat at the beginning of class then you're marked absent.

"So how's Penn?" I ask Sienna as we wait for the last bell to ring and the class continues to fill up with tired students.

"He's good," She nods. "He's having some issues with his sister but it gets complicated. Anyway, do we have plans this weekend?"

"No, I don't think so, but we should make some. Andrew's probably going to be busy all weekend with his video game thing so we should go to the movies or something," I suggest. "We need to invite a big group of people though so I'm not a fifth wheel."

"I'm sure we can make that happen," She assures me and I'm sure she's just doing it to make me feel better and it really is working. Having plans that exclude my boyfriend makes me feel better- like I'm not leeching into Andrew all of the time. The bell rings then, signaling the beginning of first period, which is when Mrs. Turner, our calculus teacher, walks through the door and begins to go over the homework.

After calculus, I part ways with Sienna and walk into the social studies wing for psychology. It's a pretty boring class because I don't really know anybody in there. None of my close friends are in that class but I do have a few acquaintances so it's not too bad, I guess.

"What's wrong with you?" I hear one of those acquaintances ask me as she joins me at our small table that fits four people. I sit at the four person table with Sara, who just sat down, her boyfriend, Benji, and Melinda, who doesn't really talk at all, she just keeps to herself. She seems nice, I guess, but I wouldn't really know since she's only said like, two words ever.

"Nothing," I sigh. "Is it really that obvious that I'm not in a good mood?"

"It's pretty obvious," She nods. "But it's nothing?"

I shrug. "Boyfriend problems, I guess. Nothing to be concerned about."

"What about boyfriend problems?" Benji pipes, sitting down across from me and beside Sara. "I have tons of those."

"Are you calling me a boy?" Sara wonders with raised eyebrows.

"No," He laughs. "I'm saying that I'm cheating on you with that guy from my algebra class."

She jokingly shoves his shoulder and they both laugh. "You two are cute and it makes me want to vomit," I mutter.

"What?" Benji wonders with another energetic laugh. Sara and Benji are just juniors but psychology is open to both juniors and seniors, so they don't really know any of my friends but I'll still invite them to the movies this weekend. The more the merrier, I guess. Anyway, getting to know them during this class, I've learned that they've been together for two and a half years, ever since the beginning of their freshman year. They're a really cute couple as well. "Don't you have a boyfriend?"

"They're fighting," Sara informs her boyfriend just as Melinda silently takes her seat beside me and then the bell rings to start class.

The teacher, Mr. Ryan, stands up from where he's sitting at the desk and greets the class. "Good morning. Pull your text books out and turn to page 74. Today, we-"

He stops talking when the classroom door opens and somebody walks in. That's really unfortunate for whoever just walked in because Mr. Ryan is a nice teacher and everything, but he is a stickler for being on time for class. However, the girl who walks in isn't anybody from this class. She has dark curly hair and a tiny smirk on her face as she looks over the class as if appraising us for auction or something.

"Can I help you?" Mr. Ryan wonders, obviously annoyed by the interruption.

"Yeah, I'm new," She tells him, looking over at the tall teacher. "Is this psychology?"

"Oh," He realizes that she's supposed to be here and then grabs a text book from his desk. "Charlotte?"

"That's me," She chirps and I suddenly start to appraise her just like she did to us moments ago. This is Charlotte Ortega, one of those new twins that's starting class today. According to what Mason said, she isn't very nice either so I'm just going to ignore her for right now.

He gives her the text book and gives her a small talk about how the class works and then we get back to class as she sits down at an empty seat across the room from my table. I can't help but notice how she looks so mischievous. Like she's just asking for unnecessary trouble.

"So, page 74. We're going to discuss Freud."

2 Movie Nights

"This was supposed to be really romantic," Andrew whines as we leave the 24 hour restaurant that we just had sundaes at.

"It is romantic," I assure him with a little giggle. "It's our first date, it doesn't have to be incredibly romantic with hot air balloons and fireworks or anything. I'm having a really good time, Andrew."

"The first date is supposed to be impressive though," He points out. "You have to let me get a redo."

"A redo?" I grin over at him with raised eyebrows. I'll just tell you what had happened earlier in the night right now before this gets confusing. It's summertime so we're in our summer schedules at the dance academy and it's Saturday night, just a few days after Andrew asked me to be his girlfriend and I said yes. So we drove in his car to a fancy restaurant in downtown Los Angeles and then, Andrew had planned to take me to the aquarium because he knows how much I love dolphins and turtles and they have a long underwater tunnel to see the sharks up close and it's really cool and open really late. Anyway, when we got to the aquarium, they said that the whole building was reserved for a private party tonight and we couldn't get in, which ruined his romantic plans. We just got out of a 24 hour diner because we bought ice cream sundaes since we have nothing else better to do and it's only eleven so we shouldn't go back to campus for a while. It's nice to just spend some alone time with him. "You don't need a redo."

"Fine," He concedes. "But you just wait until our second date. I am going to blow your mind. Now, what would you like to do now?"

"Well, since we can't be completely romantic tonight, we can be totally cheesy," I suggest as we stand beside his car and talk this through. "You know, like dinner- which is already done- and a movie."

"I can do cheesy," He grins such a beautiful grin before gripping my waist lightly in his hands and then pressing my back against the cool metal of his car behind me. He leans forward and puts his lips on mine- our third kiss of the night but really, who's counting?- and I learn forward to meet his kiss. I don't need to step onto my tippy toes thanks to the fancy heels that I'm wearing, which is something that I shouldn't get used to because most of the time, Andrew is way taller than me. We don't start crazily making out there against his car like I want to because I have a bit more class than that (this diner is a bit busy right now) and Andrew respects me too much to do that so after about twenty seconds of a slow, nice kiss, Andrew pulls away and one of his hands falls from my waist while the other one loops all the way around, pulling my right side close to his left as he leads me around the car to the passenger side. "After you, Stell."

I laugh and teasingly roll my eyes as I can now see how far he's going to take this 'cheesy date' thing. It'll be interesting how this goes. We hold hands over the console as Andrew drives down the street towards the closest movie theater. However, late night LA traffic is pretty heavy so I think it'll take a little while.

"So I'm really glad that we're doing this," Andrew speaks, looking over at me since we're in traffic and not moving so he doesn't have to keep his eyes on the road.

"Me too," I smile softly over at him as I take in how beautiful he is. I've known him for two and a half years and I never realized how beautiful he is, but he really is gorgeous. His blonde hair that is effortlessly messy on top of his head. His dirty green eyes that I can stare into for hours. His harmonious laugh that puts a smile on my face. His perfectly pink-ish lips. All of these perfect things add up to make one perfect person and not even just on the outside, he's also perfect on the inside. He's kind, thoughtful, caring, funny, sweet. He's everything. "I really think this is going to be beautiful."

"We're going to make a totally awesome couple," Andrew agrees with me, rubbing his thumb over the back of my thumb and it is such a small gesture but it feels so comforting.

"People will bow down before us at how adorable we are," I giggle jokingly. "Like Kim and Kanye or Brad and Angelina."

"Will and Jada," He adds with a small laugh. "Even Shakespeare and Anne Hathaway will be jealous of us."

"Mickey and Minnie, Barack and Michelle, David and Victoria, Ashton and Mila, Zac and Vanessa. They will all wonder how we do it. 'How do you do it?!' They will cry. 'How are you such a beautiful couple?! Show me your beautiful ways!" I joke dramatically (because, in all honesty, I do everything dramatically. I'm a drama queen and Andrew had said it was adorable).

"Wait, I thought those last two broke up a while ago? You and Mason were really mad about it and everything," Andrew says with a confused frown. The cars begin to inch up in front of us so he turns to look at the road just long enough to inch up as well, keeping up with the slow pace of the dark traffic.

"I will never give up on Zanessa," I tell him in all seriousness. "Anybody with eyes can tell that they are in love. No matter what they think right now, I just know that they will come around again. Some people are just supposed to be together. Even if they lose sight of that for a little while."

"So you believe in true love and all of that stuff?" He asks me.

"Yeah. I mean… I don't know. I believe that Zac and Vanessa are meant for each other. I don't know if I necessarily believe that every single person has a soul mate and will fall in love with the right person at the right time. But true love? Yeah, I think that if you find the right person, you can truly love somebody forever," I respond with a slight blush creeping onto my cheeks but with all of the makeup I'm wearing, I'm confident that Andrew isn't able to notice it at all. "What about you?"

"Sure," He nods. "I think it's rare, but I think that it can happen."

The traffic loosens up and it only takes us another few minutes to drive all the way down the road and into the nearly full parking lot of the movie theater. We get out of the car (Andrew opens my door for me and I suppress another mindless giggle) and we walk, holding hands, towards the doors of the theater.

"So I'm taking a rain check on the aquarium date," I inform him with a firm nod. "Because I really want to go."

"Of course," He grins at me with a nod and then leans over and kisses my temple just as we approach the box office area where we have to buy our tickets and we haven't even decided what movie we want to watch yet. "I'll take you anytime that you want."

"You're awesome," I giggle, resting my head on his shoulder with an intense amount of affection for this perfect boy.

"Duh," He scoffs jokingly. "So, what do you want to see?"

"What do you want to see? Stella?" There's a hand waving in front of my face. I blink a few times to knock myself back into reality and I look around me to see a group of my friends standing around me, looking at me in confusion.

"What?" I mutter, realizing that I was zoning out for a while there.

"I said, what do you want to see?" Mason asks me with an amused laugh but I can see the worry in her eyes.

"Oh," I say, looking up at the list of movies that are currently playing as they're listed above the box office window. "I don't care. Nothing sad. Preferably funny."

"Got it," She smiles and then turns towards the rest of our friends and they continue to converse about what movie we should see. There's a lot of us there, per my request, which was really nice of them to come. Not only was it nice of them to come but it was nice of Sienna and Mason to gather them all on such a late notice. Mason, Sienna, Penn, Spencer, Perry, Brian, Benji, Sara, Mary, Lucas, and then there's me. Mason and Brian, Sienna and Penn, Spencer and Perry, Benji and Sara- they are all couples, which leave me, Mary, and Lucas to be the only single ones there. I mean, I don't really mind it all that much because my friends don't act crazily affectionate towards their significant other while in a big group but all of the subtle hand holding and stuff like that kind of makes me sad. It shouldn't make me sad though, because I have a boyfriend, he's just not here. And yet, I'm sad anyway.

"Here, Stell," Brian chirps as he hands me a movie ticket. I didn't even know that they'd picked a movie already but I guess so because everyone is in line now, buying tickets.

"Oh, it's fine. I can buy my own, but thanks," I assure my friend with a small smile.

"Really, it's okay," He tells me. "Besides, I already bought it and I'll just make Andrew pay me back later."

I know that he feels bad for me because I'm all down in the dumps about my fighting with Andrew but it's not like I'm special or anything. Everybody fights with their boyfriend/girlfriend, I'm just such a drama queen that it affects me more than it affects most people. And it's not like I'm exactly short on cash either, but I appreciate the friendly gesture from Brian and follow everyone into the theater.

"Enjoy yourself," Sienna nudges my shoulder as she walks beside me and Penn is on the other side of her along with his two friends, Spencer and Perry. I've only met them a few times, Spencer and Perry, but they seem nice and they make a cute couple. Which is unfortunate for me right now because cute couples make me sad. I'll suck it up though, and have a good time, because my friends worked hard to get everybody here at such late notice and they did it for me.

I smile over at Sienna and relax my shoulders a bit, forcing myself to forget about Andrew for just a little bit. "I am. I promise."

"Good," She chirps. "So, we need to talk about what we're going to do for Mary's birthday, because it's coming up."

I glance over at Mary, who is having a conversation with Sara on the other end of the crowd so she can't hear Sienna talking. "Oh yeah, I forgot."

"Well, I don't think that she knows that we know that it's her birthday next weekend so I think we should totally throw her a surprise party," Sienna suggests. "We can have the party at my uncle's house and we can invite a bunch of people. It'll be fun."

Her uncle, being the owner of the Vaughn schools, is super loaded, so his house is enormous and it's the perfect place to throw a party, so I already love her idea. "That's a really good idea. We can get a cake ordered from that fancy cake place that makes pearls out of fondant."

"Such good ideas," She grins at me. "Which is why you're part of the party planning committee."

"You know that I can't pass up an offer like that," I laugh jokingly. "Of course I'll help. I assume Mason is going to help too?"

She nods as we all walk through the door into the dark theater and we find seats altogether at the very top of the theater and we have a few minutes until all of the lights go off to start the movie. "Yep. Anyway, we'll talk more about it later, just make sure that you don't tell anybody. It's top secret."

"I am a great secret keeper," I assure her. "My lips are sealed."

I sit between Sienna and Lucas in the back row of theater seats and for the rest of the time, we're all silent to watch the previews and then the movie, which is a pretty funny movie and thankfully has no romance in it what so ever. It's a major relief for me because I'm not in the mood to see other people have successful love lives when mine is walking on thin wire. I'm too selfish for that.

Once we get out of the theater, I check my phone and see that I have a missed call from Andrew so I excuse myself from the group as they all begin laughing again over the funniest parts in the movie. Leaning against a secluded wall, I put my phone to my ear after dialing my boyfriend's number.

"Hello?" He answers.

"Hey," I chirp. "You rang?"

"Yeah, where are you?"

"I'm at the movies," I inform him, trying to sound has chirpy as I can because I don't want to sound grumpy because then that might start a fight or an argument or something. I feel like talking to him is like cutting wires to a bomb. Take one wrong turn and it'll explode. That's not how relationships should be, I don't think. Andrew is only my second serious boyfriend though, so I guess I'm no expert on the subject but it just feels wrong that I'm afraid of saying the wrong thing to the person that I'm supposed to be completely open and honest with. "We just saw this really funny movie and this elephant did this thing where... you know, I think you just have to see it. What's up?"

"I thought you said that you had a chiropractor session thing today," He reminds me.

"Yeah, I did. It was right after school and then when I was done with that, a bunch of us came out to the movies," I explain to him. "Do you want me to bring you back some popcorn or something? We haven't left the theater yet."

"Wait, a bunch of you?" He repeats what I just said. "Why didn't you tell me about it?"

"I figured that you'd be busy with your video game," I mutter, unable to hide the bitterness in my voice but I think that it's okay that I'm bitter, after the week of him neglecting me for the stupid things, and I deserve to be bitter.

"I told you yesterday that we could hang out today," He reminds me.

"So I'm supposed to memorize your tight schedule so that you can squeeze me in when it's convenient for you?" I wonder sarcastically. "Because I'm pretty sure that if I asked you to come with us, you would have snapped at me for interrupting you or for forgetting about your tournament. I really can't win either way with you right now."

"It still would have been nice if you asked," He mumbles.

"Oh yes, because my favorite thing to do is to get rejected by my boyfriend every single time I ask him to do something," I mutter irritatedly. "I invite you everywhere and you say no every single time so how am I supposed to just know that you wouldn't say no this time? Because you absentmindedly mumbled to me yesterday that you were going to be free today? Why didn't you call me to invite me to do something then?"

"I'm calling you right now, aren't I?" He says, obviously as irritated as I am.

"It's 10:30!" I yelp. "We have curfew at midnight so what were you expecting to do with an hour and a half?"

"An hour and a half is kind of a long time, we could have hung out in my room or something," He suggests as if it's the most obvious thing in the world, but it's not. He says 'hung out' in a way that I recognize as the tone that he uses when 'hang out' usually means 'have sex' and that pisses me off so much.

"Oh my, gosh," I press my palms into my eyes to stop any tears from coming out as if my hands are plugs, keeping my tears in my eyes. I'm not wearing any makeup so I don't worry about smearing it but I know that my eyes will be obviously red when I return to the group after this disastrous phone call. "So that's all that I am to you now? Just somebody to fuck when you feel like you can finally pause your game? Do you seriously just expect me to be there at your beck and call and then just drop my panties for you as if everything is okay between us?"

"That's not what I meant, Stell," He sighs.

"Then what did you mean?" I snap and then I sniffle against my will but it was kind of soft so I hope that it was soft enough that Andrew didn't hear it on the other end. I used to hope that my blush was light enough to hide behind my makeup. Now, I'm hoping that my sniffle is quiet enough to hide behind the cell reception. The sad irony is not lost on me. "Because I obviously misunderstood you."

"I just don't know what you want from me right now," He admits, not even trying to hide his frustration. "First, you get mad at me for being too busy but when I'm free, you don't want to hang out and then you get mad at me for wanting to hang out. You're kind of being impossible right now, Stell."

"Yeah, well I'm not the only one," I snap at him. "You know, maybe I didn't invite you tonight because I wanted a night without you. Without fighting with you or sitting next to you as I beg you to get away from the TV just for a little bit. Maybe I'm a little bit tired of putting an exhausting amount of effort into this relationship when the only thing you're putting your effort into is moving your fingers faster on the controller. You don't even look at me when we're talking. Why should I care so much when you seem like you could care less? Do you understand how pathetic that makes me feel? Jeez, you know what I want, Andrew? I want you to want to be with me. That's really all I fucking want."

I hang up on him and then turn my phone off so that he can't call me back. I really don't want to talk to him again tonight. I'll deal with him tomorrow. That's another thing that isn't right. I shouldn't think that way about my boyfriend. I shouldn't have to deal with him, I should look forward to seeing him the next day, but I don't. I don't want to see him tomorrow because I know that the only thing that's going to happen is that we're going to fight and we are going to continue to fight until we decide to try harder or until one of us finally decides that they've had enough and that's the end of us. And my worst fear is that the latter is going to come true pretty soon.

*Picture on the side is Diana Agron, who plays Stella. Thanks for reading!

3 Monday Mopes

"How long are we going to fight before we can... uh, not fight?" Andrew asks me as we're sitting in the food court during lunch on Monday morning.

"I don't know. How long are you going to be a jerk?" I fire a question back at him.

"I'm trying my best here, Stell," He insists, leaning over the small table so that he can talk quietly to me without anybody else hearing the conversation. Our food court has different sized tables and usually, we sit in a long booth with all of our friends but today, Andrew said that he wanted to talk so we're sitting at a small two person table instead. "I honestly do not know what you want from me."

"I think it's pretty obvious what I want," I snap at him in irritation.

"Is it to break up? Because that's what it seems like right now," He grumbles.

"No, I do not want to break up," I grumble as I eat my salad. "I just want to stop fighting. I love you, Andrew, and I just wish that you'd get off of your ass and try as hard as I am. It's like you're not trying at all here."

"It's just the tournament thing, why don't you understand that?" He asks me in irritation. "After it's done, everything's going to go back to normal."

"Everything is going to go back to normal?" I wonder with raised eyebrows. "No it's not. You have been ignoring me for over a week now and I try. I try so hard to be with you but you just don't care at all. You're not trying. But you know what? Lunch is almost over so I'm going to start off to English because I'm tired of fighting. I'm tired of trying, so when you feel like being a boyfriend again, you can let me know."

"Stella, we have English together, I can walk with you," Andrew reminds me as if I don't already know that we have next period together. It used to be really cool that we had English together and we also have two periods of dance rehearsal together at the end of the day, which was also really cool at first but now, it's not as cool since we're fighting all of the time.

"I'll walk with Mason," I inform him as I stand up and walk towards the long table where my friends are sitting. The chatter in the food court is loud because of all the people eating lunch right now and it's busy so I have to push between chairs and tables a little bit but when I get to the table, Mason and Sienna, who are sitting beside each other, both smile up at me.

"Hey, how was your lunch with Andrew?" Sienna asks me as I stand by the edge of the table because I just want to get out of here, I don't want to sit down and talk with everyone right now.

"It was just like every other conversation I have with him," I sigh. "Anyway, Mase, do you want to head to class early or something? I'm gonna head out now."

"Yeah, sure," She nods. Mason has English with me too and usually, we all walk together to the academics building but like I said, I just want to get out of this slightly loud food court. Sienna has dance after lunch though, and her dance studio class is in the opposite direction as the academic building. Mason turns and gives Brian a goodbye kiss before scooting out of the booth. We both wave goodbye to our friends and she throws her trash away on our way out of the building.

"So we should all get together in the game room sometime this week and plan out May's birthday party," I suggest as we're walking through the grassy campus. There are a few people eating lunch outside or just walking around during their lunch break but for the most part, it's pretty calm outside. In about three minutes, the bell will ring and it'll be pretty hectic with everybody having to get to their classes.

"Yeah, that really needs to happen. We need to go shopping for party decorations and stuff like that too," Mason adds.

"Oh, and you just know how much I love shopping. I'm totally in," I pipe with a smile. This is one of the best things about my friends, especially Mason, is that if I don't want to talk about something that's bugging me, she doesn't push the subject. She helps me get my mind off of everything instead of insisting that we talk about it and working through it. Sienna's like that too, she understands that I don't want to talk about my problems all of the time and sometimes, I just need to get my mind off of things. I seriously have the best friends ever.

"Good, and make sure that you don't mention this to Mary. It's incredibly top secret," She warns me.

I nod in agreement. We get to the academic building but the bell still hasn't rung yet so we sit down on the bench that's right beside the doors to go inside. "Right. You don't have to worry about me telling her anything, I don't even have any classes with her so it'll be fine. I'm a good secret keeper anyway."

"Yeah, that's true. So when we-" Mason stops talking abruptly as the doors to the building open with somebody walking out. I assume she's just paranoid about the wrong people overhearing about the surprise party and spoiling it by telling Mary but what are the chances of that happening? Mary is really shy so she doesn't talk to many people. There are only a handful of people that would find a surprise party relevant enough to go babble to Mary about it. We both look over to see who is leaving the building and I blink in surprise when I see that it's those new twins. I've only met Charlotte so far and we didn't really even meet, she's just in my psychology class but we haven't spoken at all. I haven't even seen her twin yet but now they're both standing there, right outside the door. They look around for a moment and then their eyes land on me and Mason and stay there.

"So we should do all of this tomorrow, right? Don't you have a thing tonight?" I ask Mason, trying to ignore the two girls standing a little to our right.

"Yeah, that-" Mason starts to answer my question, but she's very rudely interrupted.

"Excuse me," Charlotte says. I can easily tell them apart because Charlotte has brown curly hair but her twin… I forget her name, she has straight red hair. And it's bright hair, obviously died, but it looks nice. They're unfairly pretty and I don't like it. "We need that bench."

"What for?" I ask her with raised eyebrows. I don't like her tone so if she thinks that I'm just going to get up and let her sit down just because she wants to, that's not going to happen.

"We would like to sit down. Obviously," She rolls her eyes at me as if that's the most obvious thing in the world and I hear an accent as she talks that I think sounds British but I'm not too good on accents.

"Okay, well then sit down somewhere else," I suggest, trying to sound as polite as I could but I really couldn't believe that she just expected both me and Mason to just get up like she's royalty or something. She's been her for a whole four days so if anything, it'd be the other way around but even I'm not that entitled.

"Char, really, we can go find another bench. It isn't that big of a deal," Her sister, also with an accent, speaks up with an eye roll. She seems to think that her sister's sense of superiority is misplaced and ridiculous as well.

"No, I want this one. When the bell rings, the whole campus will be crowded and I want to be near the door," Charlotte explains. "Will you please get up?"

Mason decides that it's her turn to speak up this time. "Look, we're not going to get up. I'm not sure why you think that we should have to get up so that you can sit down but it's not going to happen," She turns and gives me an 'I told you so' look because she's the one that said that she'd be just another Gianna. So yeah, she totally called this but I really wish that she was wrong. I'm definitely not in the mood to deal with a girl like that.

"Okay, who are you?" Charlotte demands.

If we weren't fighting over the bench right now, I'd definitely just roll my eyes and walk off but because she wants this bench, I obviously can't do that. "It's none of your concern," I tell her, trying to be calm about the situation even though she's completely ignorant and seemingly terrible.

"Fine, well I'm Charlotte and this is my sister, Heather. The Ortega Twins," She informs us as if she really does think that she's royalty here. She announced their names like she thought that it'd make us change our minds and get off of the bench, which it obviously didn't.

"That's not going to make us get up," I tell her with a shake of my head and then I lean back against the back of the metal bench just to stress the idea of how comfortable I am on this totally uncomfortable bench. "We will get up when the bell rings."

"Charlotte, cut it out," Her sister, whose name is Heather according to what her sister just said, tells Charlotte with another, more impatient eye roll. "You're being completely ridiculous."

"I just want to sit down," Charlotte huffs like a two year old who didn't get the kind of candy that she wanted at Walmart. "The people here are so incredibly rude."

"We're rude?" I wonder incredulously. "We are the rude ones here?"

She turns to glare at me to try and intimidate me and it really does not work. I am in such a crappy mood that no type of intimidation could work on me, especially not this new little brat who thinks that we should be at her beck and call, apparently. She opens her mouth to say something in response but before she can get a word out, the bell rings, which means that lunch is over and we have eight minutes to get to class. Both me and Mason stand up from the bench and head for the doors as Charlotte glares at us and poor Heather just sends us an apologetic frown. I feel really bad for her right now and I definitely don't blame her for her irritating sister. If people judged other people by their siblings, everybody on the planet would hate me.

"I'm Stella, by the way," I announce to Charlotte in my best bitchy voice (and my bitchy voice is very bitchy) and as I walk past her, I scuff my shoulder against hers a little. It's an immature gesture but like I said, I'm in no mood to play these stupid games. "Maybe we'll see you around."

Once we get inside of the building, all of the classrooms are spilling with students as they rush to get to their next classes. I stay close to Mason as we walk side by side down the hallway towards the English wing.

"Well, that was weird and intense," Mason pipes.

"Who even does that?" I wonder rhetorically and then I mock Charlotte in a high pitched, nasally voice with a bad accent. "'Excuse me, we need that bench.' Like no, bitch, you need a freaking attitude adjustment. I haven't wanted to punch somebody so bad since Gianna put a firecracker in our bag before the competition last summer."

"If you punch her, just make sure that you don't do it in front of the teachers or cameras. I don't want you to get expelled- especially when you're half a year away from graduating. That'd really suck," She reminds me.

"I know," I sigh. "I won't punch her, I just want to so bad. If Andrew drives me any crazier though, I might end up punching something. Maybe I should start doing boxing again on the weekends."

"So you want to work out for two hours every day during the week and then work out even more on the weekends?" Mason wonders incredulously.

I laugh and then nod. "It's relaxing, it helps me vent my stress without actually hitting anybody. I did it last year and it was nice but I quit during the summer because we literally work out all day during the summers and that's just too much but during the school year, it really does help. Do you wanna try to go with me? The trainers are really cute but it's so awesome because they're like, in their mid-twenties so they're too old which means that even if you wanted to touch, they'd reject you. So you can't cheat no matter what but the eye candy is amazing."

"No thanks, Stell," Mason laughs, teasingly rolling her eyes at me. "I'm way too lazy for that."

We arrive in our English class and sit down in our seats in the back of the room. Like my psychology class, we got to choose our seats at the beginning of the year but we have to sit in the same seat all year. As a result, I sit between Andrew and Mason, which won't be very fun today but I'll have to deal with it just like I've had to deal with it since last week when Andrew started blowing me off for his TV and his hand.

Even after Andrew comes into class and sits down beside me, we don't speak at all. It's a little bit awkward, but not really because we have to take notes the whole class period so even if we wanted to talk, we wouldn't be allowed to because Jackie, our English teacher, doesn't allow us to talk during notes. She's an incredibly amazing teacher but her two strict rules are to 1.) be on time and 2.) no talking during notes.

After English, I have anatomy, which is across the building from the English wing. Anatomy is okay but the only person I know in that class is my lab partner, Anthony, who also happens to be my brother. I consider him an acquaintance. Miss Hatfield is explaining the skeletal system to us and since we sit in the back of the room, Anthony asks me how things are going with Andrew and I just tell him that they're going fine. I don't plan on talking about my relationship problems with my brother because that would be extremely weird.

So then after anatomy, I have to go all the way across campus to the F Building, which is the dance studio where I have my dance rehearsals for the last two hours of the day. I walk with Anthony since we have our dance class together too and when we get into the studio, I go into the girls' locker room through the hallway in the back and get changed into my workout shorts, long sleeved t-shirt, and some tennis shoes for rehearsal. I sit with my brother, Brian, and Andrew before class starts and start to stretch even though when class really does start, we'll have an official stretching period.

"Mason told me what happened with you guys and those twins," Brian tells me with a teasing laugh once I sit down with them while we wait for the bell to ring.

"Those new girls?" Anthony wonders. "What happened?"

"Nothing exciting," I sigh. "But one of them is like the next Gianna as if this school just can't go without a super-bitch. The other one seems kind of nice, I guess."

"I think they're nice," Andrew shrugs.

"Do you have any classes with them?" I ask, ignoring the fact that we're fighting because we're in public. I mean, we fight in front of our friends and that's awkward enough but I absolutely refuse to fight with him in public places, especially in class. That's just embarrassing so while we're in class, I just pretend like nothing is wrong at all because that's the easiest thing to do.

"Yeah, well Charlotte is in my anatomy class and Heather is in my AP chem lab," He explains. "Oh, and Charlotte is in this class. At least, she was in here on Friday, remember?"

I do remember that but she sat on the other side of the room and paid absolutely no attention to us at all, which, looking back on it, I appreciate. "Well, Charlotte's a bitch," I say to him.

"She's really nice in anatomy," He shrugs.

"You talk to her?" I scrunch my nose up at him.

The bell rings as he nods his head nonchalantly. This day just keeps getting better and better.

Mr. Lynch is our dance instructor so when he walks into the room, we all stand up and start our synchronized stretching. Every day, he picks somebody to lead the stretches and it takes about ten minutes. I notice that Charlotte is standing a lot closer to us than she was on Friday. Actually, she's standing right on the other side of Andrew. I suddenly feel like one of those terribly jealous girlfriends and I don't like that. I don't want to feel jealous but I can't help it. She's a mega bitch but she's really pretty and she's obviously nice to people- I'm assuming that she's only nice to people with a dick- which makes me feel even more possessive but I just shoot her a dirty look that she doesn't see because she's focused on learning the stretches.

"Wait, so do you hold her left elbow with your right hand or your right elbow with your left hand?" Charlotte asks Andrew curiously and then she bats her eyes like freaking Minnie Mouse. She's blatantly flirting with my boyfriend right in front of me and I don't know if she knows that he's not available or not but something tells me that she just doesn't care.

"Um, the second one," Andrew replies nicely but he doesn't stop there. He stops stretching and then holds her left wrist in one of his hands and her right elbow in the other one and places her in the right position. I can't tell if he's just oblivious and way too nice to see that she's a tramp or if he's doing it to piss me off or maybe he wants to flirt back.

When he goes back to stretching, I clench my hand into a fist to refrain from slapping my idiotic boyfriend for what he just did. In front of everybody. I never used to be such a violent person but with all of this pent up rage, I just want to hit everybody at all times. This time, when I shoot a glare at Charlotte, she sees it and then just smirks back, knowing exactly what she's doing. So yes, she does know that he has a girlfriend and she knows that it's me and in this moment, I wish that I was a shape shifter so that I could shift into a lion and rip her head off. I wouldn't eat her because that's gross, I just want to murder her with a blood bath and a bunch of witnesses.

"You're a slut," I whisper over to my boyfriend just loud enough for him to hear.

He lets out a deep sigh. "I was just helping her. Don't overreact, Stella."

"Oh, I'm not overreacting yet but just you wait," I mumble, bending down to touch my toes. I consider jutting my ass out even more than necessary to give the guy behind me a show but I don't' do that. I have more respect than to do something like that but I want to so badly, just to piss Andrew off. However, it occurs to me that Andrew probably wouldn't even notice if I did anything like that. He doesn't notice anything that I do so he probably wouldn't even care and that thought just pisses me off even more. I still keep my butt to myself but I'm still so angry.

I'm definitely going to need that boxing.

*If you can see the image, that's River Viiperi, who plays Andrew (:

4 Party Planning

"I'm tired and I'm mad and I'm so incredibly tired of being mad," I mutter to Brian after dance rehearsals on Wednesday as we leave the building. I don't know why this Charlotte girl decided that she hates me or why she wants Andrew but all three days this week, starting with the elbow touch on Monday, she's been making excuses to talk to Andrew and apparently, they have anatomy together too and they talk a lot in that class. I hate her. I hate her so much. Anyway, I'm not walking with Andrew because he's a jerk and I refuse to talk to him today. It's not that I'm giving him the silent treatment, I just want one full day where I don't have to be mad and arguing for hours on end.

"I know," Brian nods. "But once you get through this fight, you guys will be pretty much indestructible."

"Yeah," I sigh. "Are you going shopping with us tonight?"

"Shopping for what?"

"Party stuff," I explain. "For the party this weekend and everything. We're not even going to the mall so you don't have to worry about carrying the bags or anything, we're just going to go to the party store."

"Sure," He chuckles. "I'll come with you guys."

"Cool, so-" I start to speak but when Anthony calls my name from behind me, I stop talking and turn to see him jogging towards me and Brian and then when he approaches us, he abruptly stops.

"Hey, can we talk?" He wonders.

"Yeah, I guess," I nod and then look over at Brian. "Tell Mason to wait for me. I'll catch up with you guys."

He nods at me and then glances over at Anthony suspiciously and then starts to walk away. "Okay, I'll tell her. See you soon then."

Once Brian walks away towards the dorm building where we were supposed to meet Sienna and Mason to continue our party planning right after class, I turn to look at my brother. "What's up? And can we make it quick? I have a thing."

"Yeah, it'll be quick," He assures me. "It's about Thanksgiving break. I just got off of the phone with Mom and she said that they're going Tennessee for Thanksgiving and they want us to fly out there with them for break."

"When's Thanksgiving?" I wonder, trying to think of what day today is and what day our Thanksgiving break starts on.

"Next week, Stell," He chuckles as if it's weird that I didn't know that. I've been so preoccupied with Andrew that I didn't even realize that we didn't have school for three days next week. "Do you want to go?"

"Yeah, I'll go," I nod. "Why didn't they call me too?"

He shrugs. "I told them that I'd tell you about it. I'm sure if you want to talk to them, you can just call them though. Anyway, Mom said that you can bring Andrew if you want."

"No," I say quickly. "I'm not going to do that, a vacation away from him sounds nice right now."

"Really? Okay then. Well we leave on Wednesday and that's it, so you can go do your thing now," He says before turning to walk away.

Without saying goodbye or anything, I just turn and continue on my pursuit to get to the dorm building so that we can go shopping.

Me and my brother used to be really close when we were little. We were like best friends because our parents were absolute workaholics so, being raised by a team of nannies, we naturally grew close to each other. We were really all each other had. Anyway, when we got into high school (we're twins, so we are in the same grade and everything), our parents sent us off to a boarding school so that they could quit their jobs and buy an RV so that they can travel the country without the burden of having two kids to watch out for. Anyway, my best friend came with us to Vaughn and her name was Carmen. Anthony and Carmen were dating and I didn't like that but they were both happy so I got over my hesitation and just let them be happy without any complaints. The first five months of my freshman year were pretty good. I had my best friend, my awesome brother, and I had an amazing boyfriend, James. He was in my biology class, which is how we met, and we'd been dating for a while and I was pretty in love with him. Anyway, around this time of year (November), he broke up with Carmen out of the blue. It broke her heart so terribly that she couldn't even stand to be around him so she left and went back home to Maine, which is where I'm from as well. I knew something bad like that would happen if they dated but she never believed me but Anthony would never talk to me about it- he never told me why he broke up with her. Anyway, just a few weeks after that, he started talking to Gianna and she was like a vampire to him. She possessed him, made him a completely different person. She convinced him that if he wanted to continue to go out with her, he'd have to "prove his loyalty" and to do that, he had to get James to break up with me. I'm not sure why she hated me, but she did and she wanted me out of the picture. Apparently, I spent too much time with Anthony or something. So then, Anthony told James that I had the clap. James, being a ridiculously stupid person, believed Anthony against me and assumed that I'd cheated on him so he broke up with me. I was absolutely heartbroken. I had really loved James and then he was gone in the blink of an eye just a few weeks after I lost my best friend. So not only did I lost my best friend and my boyfriend, I lost my brother to. I stopped talking to him after that, which is exactly what Gianna wanted. Anthony wanted me to forgive him. He'd text me, call me, and try to catch me before or after classes, stop by my dorm. I wouldn't have any of it though. He was so irritated that I'd stopped talking to him that he officially started going out with Gianna and they quickly became the power couple in school. I was mad at him for everything that he'd done to me and he was mad at me for cutting him out of my life so we just never got along after that. He'd been with Gianna up until last summer when a whirlwind of things began happening. First of all, Sienna showed up and Gianna decided to hate her for two reasons. The first one being that she was friends with me (we were roommates during the summer so naturally, we became friends pretty quickly) and the second one being that she's a really, really good dancer and Gianna doesn't like competition. After Sienna got there, Gianna and her goons attacked her at night, tied her up, and then threw her into the pool to leave her to drown. Anthony was there, helping them drown my completely innocent best friend. He claimed that after they threw her in the pool and everyone else left, he stayed back to pull her out of the pool because they just wanted to scare her but that's still just not okay at all. Gianna and Anthony finally broke up after that, when he realized that Gianna was cheating on him with one of his best friends. Fortunately, Gianna and all three of her sidekicks or whatever got expelled after the incident with the firecracker, so they are obviously not a problem anymore and once Anthony got rid of Gianna and realized what a parasite she was to him, he started working harder for my forgiveness. I've moved on from all of the crap that he's done in the past but we're still not as close as we used to be and I don't think we'll ever be that close again after going three years just absolutely hating each other. At least we get along now, that part is really nice.

"Okay, so we have to get a list together of what we need at the store and then we can head off," Mason says as I enter the lobby of the dorm building. Nobody asks me what's wrong or why I came in late, which I appreciate, and we just start talking like normal.

"Well, we're going to serve lunch, so we'll need plates, plastic silverware, and napkins," Sienna pipes. "And we definitely need a piñata."

"I like the way that girl thinks," I pipe, agreeing with her fabulous idea of having a piñata at the party. "And we will also need birthday balloons and streamers. Purple and black streamers because purple is Mary's favorite color."

"Candy," Brian adds. "For the piñata and just to have around. She really likes candy."

"Very true," Mason agrees, writing everything down on a long notepad. "Anything else?"

"Not that I can think of for today. Should we plan out how we're going to invite people without Mary finding out about it?" I add. "I mean, some people have a big mouth but they still should come to the party."

"We will tell them about it on Friday that way, they don't have enough time to talk to her and mess it up but I do know who you're talking about," She says. We're talking about Lucas because he really can't keep a secret worth his life so we won't be able to tell him about it or he'll blab to Mary about it pretty quickly. "But other than him, we can just keep it verbal and make sure people write down the information about it so that they remember but we can't have an official invitation or anything."

"Penn and I will be in charge of the cake," Sienna offers up. "The bakery is just outside of campus."

"Awesome, so then we need two people to do decorations and two people for food," Mason speaks up. "Me and Stella can do decorations since we're kind of awesome at that stuff and Andrew and Brian can get all of the food together."

"Oh, and should I get a DJ?" Sienna pipes. "Penn has a lot of friends in fraternities so I'm sure he knows a few good DJs."

"Yes! Oh my gosh, I totally almost forget about music," Mason grins thankfully at Sienna. "That's perfect. So are we ready to get to the store?"

The three of us nod so we all stand up off of the couches that we've been sitting on in the lobby and leave the building. The walk to the parking lot isn't too long and when we get there, we take Brian's car since it's the biggest and we have to fit four people in it.

"Wait, I should invite Andrew," I sigh. "So that he can reject me but at least he won't yell at me for not inviting him. Give me a sec."

I pull my phone out and call him. I would just text him but if he's playing his video games, he'll just ignore texts but he might pause the game or continue to play while talking on the phone if I call him.

"Hey, Babe," He answers the phone, obviously reading the caller ID to be able to tell that I'm the one calling him.

"Hey," I sigh, loving that he just called me 'babe' which he hasn't done in a while. We haven't spoken all day and maybe that's what we needed- just some space. "So we're going shopping for Mary's party this weekend. Do you want to come with us?"

"Now?"

"Yeah, now," I confirm.

"Uh, I can't," He mumbles, seemingly more apologetic than he usually is when he turns down plans.

"Yeah, I didn't think so," I sighed. "Well, I'll see you later. I love you."

"I love you too, Stella," He assures me with more affection than he's been using recently. He seems like he's in a much better mood right now and it feels good. It definitely puts me in a much better mood knowing that we just had a two second conversation without it turning into a fight. That must be a first in the past two weeks or so.

"Okay, let's go," I chirp as I put my phone back in my pocket and we all file into the car.

"So he's not coming?" Sienna wonders, sitting beside me in the backseat. "You seem a lot happier about that than usual."

"No, I'm not happy that he's not coming, it's just nice that we didn't fight about it," I explain. "I swear, that's the first conversation we've had in weeks that hasn't turned into an argument."

"See? It's the light at the end of the tunnel," Sienna grins at me, obviously almost as excited about the revelation as I am. "We told you that it would happen."

"Yeah," I sigh, looking out the window with a small smile on my face. Maybe Sienna is right. Maybe this is the light at the end of the tunnel. I sure hope so.

*I'm going to continue updating but there won't be an update schedule and the updates will be slow until I get more written. I don't want to feel stressed out about this because I have enough irl to be stressed about so I'm just going to take it easy, updating probably about every two weeks. Idk, we'll see. thanks for hanging in there tho. You're the best! <3

*Also, the picture to the side is Lucy Hale, who plays Sienna

5 Birthday Parties

It wasn't the light at the end of the tunnel. The tunnel is a lot longer than it originally seemed. I went to the party store on Wednesday with Sienna, Mason and Brian and I actually had hope for me and Andrew that we'd stop fighting. However, on Thursday and Friday, we were back to normal, fighting every time that we even said hello to each other. It's exhausting.

Today is Mary's party though, so I'm confident that today will be a good day. Even if Andrew wants to be whiney and complain about everything like he's been doing lately, I'm going to be surrounded by my friends and we're going to celebrate Mary's eighteenth birthday and it will be fun.

On Saturday morning, I go with Mason to Mr. Vaughn's house, who is Sienna's uncle. At first, it was incredibly intimidating being around the guy a lot considering he's the head guy of our school. He can throw anybody out with just a flick of his wrist and that's that. Squashed like a bug. He owns all of the Vaughn schools (Dancing, Vocal Music, Fine Arts, Instrumental) so he's a pretty intimidating person. However, after I've spent some time with him, I realize that he's actually not a bad guy. If I was as powerful as him, I would definitely abuse my power way more than he is so more power to him.

Anyway, the party is going to be outside at the pool because it's a pool party so Mason and I take the time to decorate the sunroom with streamers and balloons and on some of the balloons, we write 'Happy Birthday, Mary!' on them. The sunroom is attached to the house and it's a large room with three walls made out of class and the fourth wall is the one that's attached to the house with a door that leads into the kitchen. There's another two doors that lead outside to the stone area around the in ground pool that comes with a diving board and a twelve foot deep end. We throw some balloons outside too but we keep all of the streamers in the sunroom. We even decorate the big table that, in a few hours, will showcase a huge birthday cake that Sienna and Penn will be picking up soon.

"So, this is going awesome. Sara just picked Mary up and they're going to the movies but Sara is pretending like she doesn't know that today is Mary's birthday," Mason informs me as she's reading a text that I assume is from Sara.

"Yeah, this is awesome," I agree with a nod. On the other side of the room, there are two long tables that are going to be full of platters of food and bowls of chips and candy and everything, which Andrew and Brian are in charge of, so they should be here soon with the food as well. "And Sienna texted me a little bit ago and told me that the DJ will be here at noon."

"And you and Andrew are going to be okay?" Mason wonders as we tape streamers around the room.

"Definitely," I nod. "I mean, we're not getting along or anything but if he wants to be a jerk then I just won't talk to him during the party and then we can just fight tonight. Like we always do. It'll be great."

"How can you two still be fighting? Like, what do you even fight about anymore?" She wonders incredulously.

"It's pretty much the same thing every time. He wants to play video games all of the time, I want him to actually act like a boyfriend some of the time. And now, as if things weren't awful enough right now, he's talking to Charlotte."

"The Bitch Twin?" Mason asks me with wide eyes.

I nod and purse my lips in disgust. "Yeah. Apparently, they have anatomy together and they're lab partners. And apparently, she's really nice and 'she's new. She needs people to help her out' and all of that crap. Whenever I even bring her up, he accuses me of being jealous which might be true but seriously, he talks to her more than he talks to me and I think I have a reason to be jealous. She's a bitch but she is really pretty and apparently, pretty manipulative."

"How can he be so blind?" She wonders incredulously. "Jeez, that's so hard to believe."

"I thought so too," I mumble. "But then if I continue to press the subject, he tells me that I'm suffocating him. I should give him some space. As if I spend any time with him at all. I barely even see him anymore so I'm about as suffocating as the moon suffocates the sun. I honestly don't know what's going on with him anymore. I honestly can't take too much more of this, Mase."

"I mean, you know that I love you two together," Mason says. "And I honestly don't think that he'd cheat on you with that dirty European little brat. I mean, not all Europeans are dirty brats- I actually love Europe- but that particular girl is a dirty brat. Anyway, my point is that if you are this unhappy, maybe it is a good thing to just take a break. Once you guys have had a nice time away from each other, you'll realize how much you love each other and you'll get back together."

"I know," I sigh sadly, continuing to tape streamers around the perimeter of the room as Mason decorates the cake table with little music notes and ballet shoes of confetti. "I just don't think that if we broke up that we'd get back together and that really terrifies me."

"You will," She assures me. "You two are meant to be together, I promise you that."

"I guess we'll see," I mumble.

A little while after that, Andrew and Brian arrive with a lot of KFC, pizza, and snack food. Once Mason and I finish with the streamers, glitter, balloons and confetti, we both help them load all of the food from Brian's car onto the two long tables that are set up for food.

"When are people going to start showing up?" Brian wonders as he dumps one of the buckets of fried chicken onto a platter so that people don't have to dig through the bucket to get their food.

"I told people to be here at one," Mason tells him. "The DJ will be here anytime now and Sienna and Penn will be here at 12:30 with the cake and we'll put it over there."

I'm about to start opening the bags of chips and emptying them into the large plastic bowls but before I do, an arm snakes around my waist and I look up to see Andrew standing right beside me, using his arm around my waist to pull me closer to him. I'm surprised that he's even touching me right now because it's been so long since we've even held hands but I just go along with it because it feels nice.

"You look insanely gorgeous today," He mutters with his lips just an inch or so from my ear.

I can't hold back a small smile as I look down at my outfit- a blue skater dress with a heart cutout on the chest and white wedge heels and then underneath of that, I black bikini- and lean my head against his shoulder. I notice Mason smiling at us with what looks like a lot of relief but then she quickly looks away to give us just an ounce of privacy. "Thanks," I say quietly. "You look pretty spiffy yourself."

"I think you're lying," He chuckles. He's only wearing jeans and a t-shirt.

"Maybe," I laugh a little bit.

He kisses my cheek and I try to remember the last time that we've been this close and it's been a really long time. I want to ask him what's up with the sudden change in mood but I'm too afraid to ruin it, so I just keep my mouth shut and turn my head to press my lips to his.

"I love you," I mutter against his lips.

"I love you too, Stell," He assures me before pulling away. "We should keep working."

I clear my throat and nod in agreement. "Yeah, we should," I pipe as I walk over to the chips. Mason already has most of them open and poured into the bowls but I grab the blue bag of Doritos and open them up, pouring them into the bowl. Brian left the room to go meet the DJ at the front door so it's just us three in the room. As I grab the next bag of chips to open, Andrew starts to speak.

"Oh, and I hope it's okay that I invited the Ortega Twins," He pipes as if it's no big deal and just as he says that, I'm opening the bag and I'm so surprised at what he just said that I grip the bag way to tightly and pull against the bag, causing the chips to explode with a loud pop and then they're flying everywhere. Mason and Andrew are looking at me in surprise and I'm looking down at the floor, going over what Andrew just said to make sure that I didn't misunderstand him but I'm pretty sure that I heard him right.

"No, that's not okay," Mason shakes her head but she's eyeing me warily, gauging my reaction bit I'm just biting my lip, looking down at the floor, and trying to stay calm. "Why would you do that? Did you get hit in the head with something extremely hard or something? Like a meteorite maybe?"

"They don't know anybody," Andrew defends. "I felt bad. They're new and they don't have any friends."

"That's because at least one of them is an incredible bitch," Mason informs him. "Nobody wants to be her friend. Stella, are you okay?" She asks me, realizing that I haven't moved a muscle since the chip bomb just went off.

"I'm going to go get a broom," I say, looking up at her before turning and going into the house. Mr. Vaughn has a closet full of cleaning supplies in the main hallway so I go in there and grab the broom and the dust pan but instead of going back outside immediately, I stand in the doorway of the closet and I can feel my heart start to beat faster and my chin start to crumple but I'm not going to cry. Not at this party for one of my good friends. If I want to scream and get mad and cry then I'm going to have to wait until after the party. I carefully wipe right under my eyes to make sure that no tears had fallen and then I shut the closet door, tell myself to toughen up, and then I start walking back outside. Maybe that's why he was being so boyfriend-ish, because he was trying to butter me up for that little tidbit of information. I can feel him slipping out of my hands right now. The only two options right now are to either 1.) let him go or 2.) get pregnant and I'm not crazy enough to go for number two. I don't even think I'd be able to get him to sleep with me anymore even if I wanted to.

"Brian will clean up the chips," Mason assures me when I get back into the chip-covered sunroom. She takes the broom and dustpan from me and then shove them into her boyfriend's arms, who looks very confused considering he wasn't there when the chip thing happened. "We have to go help the DJ pick out a playlist."

Andrew is just sitting in the corner of the sunroom, opening bags of candy for the last of the bowls on the table and I want to take the broom back and start beating him with it but I don't. I'm just going to ignore him until I don't have to bottle up all of my emotions.

"Why would he do that?" I hiss as we start walking towards where the DJ is setting up in the corner of the green yard.

"I don't know," She mumbles in response.

"It's like he wants to break up," I say. "He knows that I hate her."

"I told him to uninvite them but he can't get ahold of them," She explains.

"Yeah, right," I snort. "He just doesn't want to uninvite them. Who knows? He might get lucky tonight."

"You know that he's not like that," Mason reminds me.

I don't respond to that because we reach the DJ so I introduce myself and Mason does the same before he shows us his laptop and we start to pick out songs for a good playlist.

When Sienna shows up with Penn, Mason fills her in on what happened with Andrew while all three guys work on getting the cake from the car all the way back here to the table. They came a little late, so it's 12:45 and the early birds are starting to get here but Sara and Mary aren't supposed to get here until 1:30 so we have a little bit of time until that happens. Sienna is about as surprised and angry as Mason is but I'm not going to talk to them about it right now with all of these people about to arrive. We start greeting the guests and explaining to them how we're going to hide and when we're going to jump out and yell 'surprise'. Mary thinks that Sara and her are just coming over to go swimming with Mason and Sienna, she doesn't know that there's a party because according to Sara, she still thinks that everybody forgot about her birthday.

When 1:30 rolls around, I haven't spoken to Andrew. The twins haven't shown up. Sara has just texted that they're on the way to the house. The backyard is full of people from school, ready to celebrate Mary's eighteenth birthday.

"Everybody hide!" Mason starts yelling and then everybody starts hiding in their spots. I hide along the side of the house beside Mason and Sienna although they don't have to hide because Mary is expecting both of them to be here, it's just fun to play along.

We sit in silence for a minute before we hear the door opening and then two people walking out and Sara talking and then all at once, everybody jumps out of the shadows and shouts a loud 'SURPRISE!', causing Mary to jump like she's on a pogo stick and then she starts gaping at all of us as we start cheering and clapping.

"You're all jerks!" She tells us but she's laughing and clutching her chest, obviously not expecting this at all which means we did an awesome job at hiding it from her. Lucas didn't even tell her, which is a major relief.

"You didn't really think we'd forget, did you?" I wonder with a small grin as I pull her into a quick hug.

"Yes, I really did," She nodded and then she saw the table of food. "Oh my gosh, there's candy."

She makes a bee line for the bowls of her favorite candy and I stand around talking and laughing with all of the people around me. These are some really great people and I'm not going to let Andrew and his stupidness ruin this party for me. The DJ is playing the playlist we picked out and people are being pushed into the pool or they are willingly jumping in, and others are taking advantage of the free food (Sienna) but everyone is having a good time, which is a really big relief. There's a few huge blow up balls floating around in the pool that people are tossing around and I'm talking to Mason near the sunroom but outside in the sun about how well the party turned out.

"You're a genius," I tell her with a small laugh.

"You're right, I am," She concedes. "I'm thinking about being a party planner or at least going to college for hospitality."

"Really? That's great," I grin at her. Although she could get into almost any school in the country for dance, Mason doesn't want to pursue a career in dancing so she's looking elsewhere for a career. She just hasn't figured out what exactly it is that she wants to do yet.

"Hey," Andrew interrupts our conversation with a frown on his face that makes it obvious that he's not happy about something. I'm tempted to just walk away to avoid fighting right now, but I don't want to be that immature and I know that he'll just follow me.

I look up at him and cock my head to the side. "What?"

"The security guy isn't letting Charlotte into the party," He tells me. Because Mr. Vaughn is at a conference in New York, he can't be here to watch the party so he hired a security guard to be here and look over everything instead so after Mary got here, he started watching the front door with a list of names of the people that are allowed into the house and into the party. Mason wrote the list up but she obviously didn't put the Ortega twins on that list.

"Bummer," I say, not even trying to pretend to be upset about that fact.

"Stella, seriously?" He wonders exasperatedly. "There is nothing going on between me and Charlotte, okay? I'm just trying to be nice to her. Grow up."

I glare at him but I'm now wearing sunglasses, so he doesn't know. So then I lift my sunglasses off of my face and put them on top of my head. "Fine," I sigh. "I'll see what I can do."

I walk away from Mason and walk with Andrew around the house to the front porch.

"Be nice, Stella," Andrew warns as we approach the security guard, who I recognize as Charles because he sometimes drives me, Sienna, and Mason around when we're with Mr. Vaughn. Standing across from him, Charlotte is standing with her arms crossed and an irritated scowl on her face.

"I'm always nice, Andrew," I fire back, the sarcasm dripping from my voice as I smile at the guard "Hey, Charles."

"Oh, good," Charlotte grins at Andrew. "Okay, can you please tell him to let me into the party?"

"Sorry to interrupt," I interrupt her. "But he can't let you in. Me and Charles, we're friends, and he's not going to listen to Andrew. He's going to listen to me," I explain to her as I stand beside Charles and we share a fist bump because Charles is a really cool guy.

"Okay, well tell him to let me in then," She sighs, obviously irritated at my theatrics.

"Where's the nice one? I would have let her in," I inform Charlotte, referring to Heather, who I don't know at all but she seems way nicer than Charlotte in every way possible.

"She didn't want to come," Charlotte rolls her eyes at me.

"Stella, just tell him to let her through, it's not that big of a deal. We already talked about this," Andrew speaks up, just as annoyed at my attitude as Charlotte.

"No, you talked," I remind him. "I told you that she was a vapid bitch and that I don't like her and then you invited her to my friend's party. That doesn't make any sense to me."

"You're really starting to piss me off," He grumbles quietly so that Charlotte can't hear him.

"Oh, I'm just now starting to?" I wonder with raised eyebrows, doing my best to not look affected at all by any of this. "That's completely upsetting considering the fact that you've been really pissing me off for the past few weeks. I have a lot of making up to do."

"This is ridiculous, I obviously know them!" Charlotte grumbles angrily at Charles.

"Okay, you know what? I'm not an unreasonable person," I decide, turning my attention back to Charlotte and I remember all of the times through the past week that she's made a pass at my boyfriend and she'll smirk over at me while doing it. This is my small victory and I'm going to take it for all that it's worth. It probably bugs her so badly that she isn't invited to this party, being the social savvy girl that she is. "So here's what we'll do. If you can tell me the full name of the person that this party is for, how old he or she is turning, and his or her hair color, I'll let you in. This party is for my friend and if you don't know my friend then it doesn't make any sense at all for you to be here."

"Stella," Andrew starts to speak up but I just hold my hand up and he stops talking. It's such a bitchy way to get somebody to stop talking but I'm in bitch mode right now so I don't care.

"Ten seconds," I say but Charlotte just rolls he eyes again and remains silent for the whole ten seconds. "Yeah, that's what I thought. Have a safe drive home."

"What the fuck is your problem right now?" Andrew snaps at me, pretty angry about my cold dismissal of Charlotte.

"My problem is that you think that I'm going to let you mess around with that whore right in front of me. No. If you want to fuck her then you can just leave with her and do it somewhere else," I inform him.

"I told you that nothing is happening between us," He informs me with a glare.

"Yeah," I snort in disbelief. "Well you might want to tell that to her because even a blind man could tell that she doesn't need help stretching that much. If she's been dancing for years, I'm sure she can handle a few simple stretches without you having to cradle her shoulders or that she swivels away from you to touch her toes so that you can see her invisibutt. Maybe you're right. Maybe I am jealous but that doesn't mean that I'm going to let her into this party just so that she can flirt with you."

"You know, I feel like I'm causing too much trouble, I'm just going to go," Charlotte speaks up, still standing there, listening to our argument instead of leaving.

"No," Andrew says at the same time that I say, "Yes, please."

He glares at me but I just shrug like I am incredibly indifferent about anything. I'm in 100% bitch mode now. "I'm not going to let her in. If you really want to, you can go get Sienna or Mason but do you really think that they're going to side with you over me? We're the only three people that Charles will listen to so good luck convincing one of them to let her in. Now, you can either go with her or you can come back to the party, I really do not give a flying rat's ass but just stop talking to me."

I turn around and walk off of the porch, back towards the party. A few minutes later, Andrew turns the corner too, returning to the party but we don't speak at all. I'm beyond pissed at him and he's beyond pissed at me so it's best for everyone if we just don't talk right now.

"How'd that go?" Mason wonders when I return to her.

I give her a look that pretty much answers her question and in just one moment, it's clear to me that me and Andrew are pretty much out of fuel. Our fight is done. It's all over.

6 Fighting

Every couple has a first and a last fight and they both have an incredible significance in completely different ways. The first one is kind of the starting point for the real relationship. It is the end of the Cupcake Phase which, in some ways, is kind of sad, but it's also kind of cool. It's a nice feeling, in a way, when you make up because it's like 'wow. We're a real couple now' and there's a feeling of invincibility, like you think that you and the other person can make it through anything now that you've made it through a fight.

My and Andrew's first fight was about meeting his parents about a month into our romantic relationship.

"But why don't you want to meet them?" Andrew wonders with a small sigh that only hints at the beginning of some irritation. I feel bad because I don't want him to be irritated at me but I don't know what I can do at this point to make it better again.

We're sitting in his dorm room on a Saturday and it all started when he told me that his parents were coming to visit from where they live in New Mexico so it's kind of a big deal considering he obviously doesn't see his parents that much. At first, he's irritated because I don't immediately get excited for the arrival of his parents and that's because I don't necessarily see the value in parent-child relationships. The closest thing to a parent I ever had was Mrs. Rita, who was my nanny during elementary school and helped me with my homework sometimes or Miss Sandy who was my middle school science teacher who had to explain why I was bleeding out of my hoo-ha and she also bought me my first pack of pads. Basically, I don't like parents. So then, when he invited me to go to dinner with him and his parents, I immediately declined the offer and now, he's a little bit upset about that.

"They're really important to me, obviously, and you're really important to me- that is also obvious- and I just want you to meet my parents. They don't come around all that often so you won't get the chance again anytime soon," Andrew explains again, obviously very set on the issue although I still can't tell why it's such a big deal to him.

"But I don't like parents," I say (not realizing at the time that I was quoting Grease but I understand that now), sitting on the edge of his bed as he stands up with his arms crossed, continuing to get even more irritated, which I don't want to happen. I don't want to upset him at all, I just don't think that it's a good idea for me to meet his parents.

"It wouldn't go well," I say with a shrug. "I don't know how to act around adults at all."

"Just talk to them like you talk to your parents," Andrew suggests. "They're really nice, I promise. It's not as nerve-wracking as you'd think."

"Andrew, I don't talk to my parents," I remind him sheepishly. "I mean, I call them sometimes but I don't know how to talk to adults, especially not parents and especially not my boyfriend's parents."

"You could at least try," He sighs. "Like I said, they're really cool and it's just dinner."

"I don't want to mess this up, though," I insist. "I want to wait so that I know that if I mess up my first impression with your parents, you won't hate me and run for the hills or start to think that this is a bad idea or something."

"Do you really think that I'd do that?" He wonders with wide eyes that mix with what look like anger and hurt. "Stella, I really want you to get along with my parents because like I said, all three of you are so important to me and it'd be really amazing if you liked my parents and if they liked you but even if that doesn't happen, that doesn't mean that I'm going to stop loving you."

I smile a little bit because it was only a week after we had first said 'I love you' to each other and so I still grinned like an idiot every time he even mentioned the 'love' word. "I still don't know," I mumble, afraid to humiliate myself in front of Andrew's parents. This wasn't only important to Andrew- I wanted his parents to like me as well. I really did and I was afraid that if I did this too early or if I did it wrong and messed it up.

"Does that mean that you won't let me meet your parents if they stop by?" He wonders, turning the conversation against me again.

"They won't stop by," I say with a humorless laugh. "Andrew, I don't even think my parents know that they still have kids, okay? Sometimes, yeah, they visit but they haven't done that since sophomore year. That's my whole point. I don't know the first thing about dealing with parents."

"You haven't seen your parents since sophomore year?" Andrew asks me with raised eyebrows.

"Yeah, but that's not my point. My point is that even if they did come around, I wouldn't let you meet them. They're incredibly cold people and I can guarantee you that it would not go well."

"Okay, well I guess that I can understand that but my parents are different, so please come to dinner with me? Please?"

I close my eyes and I know that I am going to regret what I'm about to say but I have to say it anyway because I'll honestly do anything to make Andrew happy. I love him. "Fine. I'll go but if anything goes wrong, I'm blaming you forever."

He smiles at me and then walks over to me, bending over and pressing his lips to mine. "I love you, you know." We kiss like that for a while before I take the hem of his t-shirt in my hands and pull up. He stands up straight and effortlessly slides the shirt over his head before we fall back onto his bed with our lips pressed together.

The dinner the week after that with his parents went extremely well. His dad is really funny. His mom is incredibly nice. Andrew is their only child so they absolutely adore him and they welcomed me with open arms. It was really nice and I've met them a few times since that but Andrew has never met my parents at all.

Anyway, the last fight of a relationship is much different than the first. Of course, there are the lucky few that don't experience the last fight. They get married and the only time they come across their last fight is when one of them dies of old age but most people aren't that lucky. The last fight is something that most couples go through and it ends most relationships. It is cold and loud and frustrated and terrible. There's a lot of frustration, yelling, crying and then, at the end when both people realize that it's over, it's quiet and sullen. It's over.

"Stella," Andrew says quietly on Sunday morning. "Wake up."

I'm already awake but I've been laying in my bed for about an hour and when I heard Andrew walk into my dorm just a few moments ago, I closed my eyes and pretended to be asleep in hopes of him just giving up and leaving me alone but that's obviously not going to happen since his hand is on my shoulder and he's softly shaking me. I don't want today to happen because I don't want this conversation to happen, which is why I've been in bed for so long.

"What?" I mumble into my pillow with a yawn. I slowly sit up in my bed, dreading the conversation that I know is coming but I also know that there is no more prolonging the inevitable. I'm not just going to blatantly give up though, maybe yesterday was a wakeup call for Andrew and he now realizes that he's pushed me to the brink and he wants to keep trying but not like we've been doing. Maybe he wants to try harder now.

"We need to talk," He tells me softly, sitting down beside me to prepare for the big talk that he also knows is about to happen.

"I know," I nod, chewing on my lip as the nerves start to shake inside of me.

"What happened yesterday was completely unnecessary," He says, shooting me a hard look as if he was my parent, scolding me for throwing a tantrum or something.

"Yeah, I agree," I say, only I'm not referring to my confrontation with Charlotte, I'm talking about how Andrew even invited her in the first place and I'm pretty sure that Andrew understands that.

"You can't tell me who to be friends with or who not to be friends with," He begins with a shake of his head. "That's not fair at all because you have a lot of guy friends."

"I have never tried to dictate who you're friends with," I defend. "You have female friends and I'm totally okay with that because I trust you, and that's not why I wouldn't let Charlotte into the party."

"Most of my friends are your friends too though," He says. "So it makes sense that you're okay with me being friends with those girls because they're your friends too. But just because you don't like her doesn't mean that I can't be friends with her, Stell."

"I never said that you couldn't be friends with her!" I exclaim. "I just think it's incredibly rude of you to invite this girl to a birthday party for a girl that she doesn't even know. It just makes it worse that I hate her. I never had a problem with you being friends with her at all. I mean, okay, that's not true, I hate that you're friends with her because she makes passes at you and you go along with it even if you might not realize that you're doing it. Anyway, I wouldn't have tried to stop you from being her friend. I respect your decision to be friends with whoever you want to be friends with even if I hate her."

"They are both new- they don't know anybody, I was just trying to be nice," Andrew tells me.

"Well, you could have introduced her to people around school and I mean, she does have classes with people that she can meet, you didn't have to invite her to this party," I say as I can feel a pressure begin to grow in my chest and I press my hand to my head so that I don't start getting too emotional.

"Why are you getting so angry over this?" He asks me, obviously irritated. "It's not a big deal and I think that you know me well enough to know that I would never cheat on you."

"Andrew, you spend more time with her than you do with me," I point out. "And the only time that you even act like a boyfriend is when you did something that you know is wrong. Before the party and come to think of it, when we went shopping and I called to invite you, you were overly nice. Was that because you did something too?"

He purses his lips and looks up at the ceiling so I know that I'm right and even though I don't want to cry, I'm about to.

"That's just great," I mutter. "The only time that you can actually be a freaking boyfriend is when you're acting like a terrible boyfriend. Wonderful. That's so fucking pathetic, do you realize that?"

"We were just in her dorm playing this video game that isn't out yet here but they have it in Europe and it was really cool but I knew that you'd get mad so I didn't want to tell you. But you know that I'm a good boyfriend, Stella, and I would never do anything to hurt you."

"A good boyfriend?" I wonder hysterically as I stand up from my bed and my blood starts to boil. I can feel the fight about to ensue and I don't like it one bit. "Every single thing that you have done in the past few weeks has hurt me, Andrew. I'm not even sure that you knew that we were still dating these past few weeks. I have tried everything. I invite you everywhere I go, I hang out with you in your dorm but you're so distant all of the time. You won't even hold my hand anymore, Andrew."

"I've just been distracted a little bit but that doesn't make it okay for you to act like a brat like this!" He snaps.

"I am not acting like a brat!" I yell at him before I remember how thin the walls are here so if we start yelling, we'll eventually get yelled at if people start complaining about the noise, which I don't want to happen. I can feel tears start to spill over my eyelids and down my cheeks but I know that it's about to flow like a waterfall so I don't even try to wipe them away. "Just because I don't let you walk all over me all of the time does not mean that I'm being a brat. It means that maybe I want to spend some time with my boyfriend occasionally. Maybe I want to go out to dinner sometimes and maybe, God forbid, sometimes I even want to do dirty things with him without it being the only thing we do. Like, the only time that you wanted to hang out was just to hook up and that's so disgusting. I don't get how I'm just a doll to you now or something."

"We were both wrong here," Andrew states quietly. "You can't just throw all of the blame onto me like that."

"How is your monotonous attitude my fault? Am I not pretty enough for you? Am I boring now? Like, what did I do wrong for you to stop wanting to be with me? How is it my fault? Please tell me, Andrew."

"You know that's not what I meant," He mumbles.

"No, I think that's exactly what you meant," I snap at him angrily and then I lose it. I start crying which makes my bones start to shake but I don't want to sit down beside Andrew so I sit down in my desk chair and I continue to cry a lot. Usually, I make it a point not to cry in front of people but this is a special situation and I just don't care anymore. "I can't do this."

"Do what?" He wonders.

"This fighting," I cry pathetically. "I am so tired of it. I'm tired of everything. We used to be good together. We were perfect but you've turned into such an ass. Maybe I've changed too, I don't know. I am so tired of being the only person trying here. You act like you don't even care and I have tried my best to push through it until you start to care again but I'm tired and I'm done, Andrew. You make me feel like shit all of the time and I just can't feel like this anymore."

"You're... done?" Andrew wonders as his eyes widen with shock as if he really didn't expect me to say something so drastic. As if he thinks that he can do whatever he wants- treat me however he wants and I'm just going to sit there and take it without doing anything about it. He should know me better than that.

"Why do you even care? You haven't cared for weeks but now that you realize that I'm not going to just sit down and take it, you suddenly care again? Well, then say something to make me change my mind. But you won't do that, because it requires effort and that's something that you just don't do anymore. Not when it comes to me."

"So you want to break up?" He asks me, biting his bottom lip to try and hide how upset he is but I can tell. I can tell that even big, tough Andrew is also on the verge of tears right now although they will never fall and he will never admit it. His eyes start to dart around my face, searching for anything that might hint at me joking or taking back what I'd just said as he begins to panic but I won't back down.

"We both knew that this was coming," I cry, my heart pounding terribly in my chest. "What did you think was going to happen when you came in here this morning?"

"I don't know, I thought that we could talk through this Charlotte issue but I didn't think that you'd want to break up, Stella. That's incredibly drastic, so just calm down for a minute and think about it, okay?"

"Charlotte isn't the only issue here. It's Charlotte. It's your stupid video games. It's how you find excuses to avoid talking to me when you used to find excuses to start talking to me. It's how I always have to text you first because you can't be bothered to pick up the phone. It's how I have to be afraid of what to say next because I'm afraid of making you mad. It is everything."

"Stella, I never meant to hurt you," Andrew says quickly, trying to find the right thing to say to make me change my mind but I'm not so sure there is anything to be said anymore. I think we've said all that there is to say.

"I know that," I nod in all honesty. "And I love you so much but it's just not working anymore and we both know that. I'll go insane if we keep up with all of this fighting all of the time. I just can't take it anymore."

"Babe,"

"Please get out of my room," I interrupt him, not wanting to hear him beg for my forgiveness again because I seriously cannot take it right now. Breaking up with him was one of the hardest things I've had to do in a really long time and I don't want him to continue to make it harder. "Just leave me alone for a little while. Maybe we can be friends again after a break but right now, I just don't want to see you."

He opens his mouth to say something but then it's like he realizes that there's nothing he can say that'll make me change my mind anymore so he just sighs, stands up, and walks over to me. I'm still crying pretty hard so he bends down and kisses the top of my head. "I really love you, Stella."

And then he's gone.

Hey! So it's been a while since I've done a plug for my info, so if you ever wanna get a hold of me or something, here's a few places that you can go. I think it'd be really rad if you guys went to my Tumblr because there, I'll post (and have been posting) a lot of teasers and extra stuff about the story and other stories that I've written so please check it out!

My ask is: http://ask.fm/writerbug44 My tumblr is: http://young-lost-desperate.tumblr.com/ My Twitter is: https://twitter.com/Writerbug44 My other Wattpads: @writerbugsecrets for teasers for story ideas and R rated scenes from other stories and short stories... @writinghelper for writing tips and an FAQ

7 Broken Hearts

Two days. I just have to get through two days of school and then we're free for Thanksgiving break and I will be across the country with my family that I never see. It will be uncomfortable and irritating most of the time with old aunts pinching my cheeks and uncles claiming that they feel so old because I'm about to graduate high school, but at least it'll get my mind off of Andrew and how we broke up yesterday.

Pulling myself out of bed on Monday morning is almost impossible. All of my limbs feel like they weigh a ton and my head aches from all of the crying, but I have to get to class. If Sienna and Mason didn't come barging into my room twenty minutes before class started, however, I'm sure that I wouldn't have been able to make it on time because I was still sitting in bed, waiting for the heaviness of my body to wear off but it never did.

"I didn't shower," I mumble as Mason pushes a pile of clothes into my arms.

"There's no time," She tells me. "You smell fine so just get dressed and hurry."

"Fine," I sigh, realizing that I didn't get up in time to go for a run this morning, which is something that I do every morning. I guess I slept through my alarm though, because I don't even remember waking up to turn it off or anything.

Sienna kindly ushers me into my bathroom and closes the door behind me so that I can get dressed out of my pajamas that I've worn for over 24 hours now. After I ended things with Andrew yesterday morning, I never changed out of my pajamas. Instead, I just called Mason, who came over right away with Sienna and we all stayed in my room all day while I pigged out (which is something that I rarely ever do) on ice cream and popcorn and Sienna even ordered pizza and I ate a lot of it. I also cried a lot and watched sad movies and then cried some more. It was a rough day.

Today, my face is sticky with tears and I think there's crumbs nesting in my ratted hair but I brush them out since I don't have enough time to shower. In the bathroom, I get dressed in the sweatshirt that Mason handed me that's gray with a black lipstick kiss print on the front and my favorite pair of jeans. They are really comfortable and not too tight but they still look kind of cute. I'm too tired to put on real shoes though, so I just slip on my Ugg slippers and pull my hair up into a mess bun.

"How terrible do I look?" I wonder with a yawn as I grab my bag ten minutes later to head for the academic building and one of the toughest days that I've been through in a while. I'm already considering the option of skipping English today.

"Not so bad," Sienna assures me as they both push me out of the room and into the hallway that's now empty since most people are already on their way towards class. We have a little less than ten minutes to get there so the only way we'll make it on time is if we speed walk, which is hard on my heavy feet but I don't want to make my friends late so I push through it and keep up with their frantic pace.

"I'm sorry if I make you guys late," I speak up as we're halfway through campus.

"We don't mind," Mason assures me. "How are you feeling today? Any better?"

I think for a minute. Ever since they pulled me out of bed this morning, I haven't really given myself any time to think about how I'm feeling on this gloomy morning, so I speed walk and think at the same time. That ache in my chest is still there like a black void where a chunk of my heart used to be. My eyes still feel heavy and swollen, holding back a heavy dam but doing a much better job at holding it back.

"Not really," I finally decide. "I'm not collapsing into a puddle of tears though, so I guess that's an improvement."

"Are you sure you'll be okay with seeing him today?" Sienna asks sympathetically from my right side. We enter the academic building with five minutes to go so I'm confident that we'll make it on time but we continue to speed walk just in case.

"I don't know," I respond honestly. "It'll definitely suck."

"Well, it'll be fine," Mason pipes optimistically- too optimistically, actually. We approach the hallway where I have to split from Mason and go with Sienna to Calculus. "Just text me if you need anything- I'll be there in a jiffy no matter what."

Before I can say anything, she's hurrying down the hallway and Sienna, with her elbow hooked onto mine, is pulling me towards our classroom so that we can make it there on time.

"Seriously, Stell, how are you feeling?" Sienna wonders as we get into the classroom and then right after we sit in our seats, the bell rings for class to start. We made it on time.

I shrug. "I feel like there's a hole the size of Texas inside of me and it hurts like hell but what can I do about it now? It's over so I just have to deal with it and then move on. I'm sure that I'll feel better eventually."

She sends me a sympathetic smile as Mrs. Turner begins her lesson on tangent, sine, and cosine stuff that I already learned sophomore year in trigonometry. Since I already know all of this stuff, I decide to rest my head on the desk and maybe I'll sleep or just lay here for a while because Mrs. Turner is one of those teachers that doesn't care if people sleep in her class but she won't repeat anything or go over it again if you ask her and she knows that you were sleeping or something. "It's your own fault" she says, but since I already know this stuff, I don't mind just laying my head down and ignoring her math talk while I worry about the raging headache I have right now.

Psychology and choreography go by in a complete blur. Charlotte is in my psychology class but my back is turned to her and I'm ignoring her existence. It's not like she's the reason that I broke up with Andrew but she sure did facilitate it and I just really hate that girl so much.

After my first three periods, it's time for lunch, which is something that I'm dreading due to the fact that I have lunch with Andrew and all of my friends. Maybe Andrew won't be there- maybe he'll go eat somewhere else or something, but I don't think that's going to happen considering my friends are his friends too.

I'm proven right when I buy my salad and then approach the large table that I sit at with all of my friends and Andrew is there, sitting on the edge beside Brian.

Everyone at the table shoots me a sympathetic frown and then starts glancing between me and Andrew, waiting for what's about to happen. I avoid looking at Andrew at all costs as I sit down across from Sienna on the other side of the table and eat my salad.

"Are you okay?" Sienna asks me in a whisper so that nobody else can hear it except for Mason, who is sitting to my left.

I shrug and nibble on my salad. "I'm better than I thought that I'd be. I'm also pretty sure that by the end of the day, I'll be a puddle of tears but I'm hoping that I can hold that off until I get back to my dorm after school."

"We'll be there for you," Mason assures me with a nod.

"You should go be with your boyfriend, Mase," I tell her.

She shakes her head at me. "No way. We have all thanksgiving break to spend with each other. Besides, Brian is going to be with Andrew, doing about the same thing that we're going to be doing only in a more masculine way."

"Right," I sigh.

"Sorry. I shouldn't say his name, I won't do that again," She tells me apologetically. "Do you want me to go talk to him? Because I'll go talk to him if you want me to."

"No, it's fine. I don't really want anything to do with him for a while," I say. "I mean, you're still friends with him. You guys can go hang out with him if you want, I'm just going to keep my distance."

"Yeah, we totally understand," Sienna nods. "Whatever you want, we totally support you."

"Unless you want to shut us out, because I read that people do that and that's not okay with me," Mason adds. "But other than that, we totally support whatever you want to do."

"I would never shut you guys out," I tell them. Just the thought of surviving this without my two best friends just makes me sick. I'd never be able to go through this alone.

All through lunch, I talk to Sienna and Mason about stupid stuff- anything we could think of to get my mind off of Andrew, who is still sitting on the other side of the table from us but I refuse to even glance in his direction. It just hurts too much.

And the worst is still to come because right after lunch, I have English with Mason and Andrew and I sit right next to Andrew.

"I think I'm just going to skip," I tell Mason as we walk down the hallway together towards the classroom.

"You shouldn't do that," She tells me. "I know that it's really going to suck and it'll be really hard, but it'll make you look like a bigger person if you show up. And who knows? Maybe he'll skip anyway."

I hate that she's right- if I skip, I'll look weak and I don't want to do that. I know that Andrew saw me at lunch so he'll know that I'm fine and I'm just skipping English to avoid him. I have too much pride to admit how much this breakup is affecting me, although I'm sure he already knows that it's killing me. Without any signs from me at all, he still knows me and he knows that I'm over dramatic about everything.

"Stella, you'd need stitches if you got a paper cut," He'd told me once in a fit of laughter after I was hysterical about the ending of some sad chick flick.

He knows that this is killing me regardless if I show up to English or not. However, my pride will deny the fact that he already knows because I will refuse to admit my pain to him in any way and if I skipped English, it'd be like admitting to him that he's killing me inside.

"Yeah, I'll go," I mumble, biting my lip to stop myself from crying or panicking or both. I have no idea how I'm going to face him. "But I'm going to hate it."

We walk into the room and I'm a little bit relieved when Andrew isn't there and I feel a glimpse of hope that he won't show up. Just like he knows me, I know him and I know that he's hurt by the breakup too. Even if he stopped acting like he cared about me in the past few weeks, I know that he really does care and he is hurt too. Hopefully, he will find it in himself not to come to English today.

I fold my arms on the desk and rest my head on them, completely exhausted and only halfway through the day. Closing my eyes, I hear Mason shuffling around in her bag beside me as she gets her English stuff out but I'm just too tired to even sit up so I'm going to just listen to Jackie today. She's so cool that she doesn't really care if we lay our heads down during class. She really doesn't care about what we do as long as we aren't disrupting the learning of others and we're on time for her class. I'm not going to sleep though, because I need to pass this next test, but when she's giving notes, I'm just going to listen and absorb and then, if I still don't get it, I'll copy down Mason's notes later.

My head is facing Mason but I can still tell that Andrew has arrived because I hear his chair squeak slightly as he pulls it out and then sits down. I keep my eyes closed and pretend that I'm dead. That's the only way that I'll survive this hour of class. I'm just going to completely ignore him and pretend that he just doesn't exist or anything.

That works for the whole hour. I sit there unmoving while I listen to Jackie talk about Shakespeare and all of his wonderful plays that nobody understands because of his weird yet oddly romantic English.

Once the period is over, I stand up and immediately turn my back to Andrew, facing Mason as we walk out of the room before I even have the chance to see him in my peripheral vision. I just don't want to see him at all right now.

"Okay, so that wasn't that bad but I'm pretty positive that I'm going to be skipping dance today. Charlotte is in that class and so is Andrew and I just really don't want to go. I can't just put my head down and ignore the world while I'm dancing," I explain to Mason even though I know that she'll talk me out of skipping.

And she does. By the time that we part ways and I am on my way to Anatomy, she has me convinced that I need to go to practice today. I have no idea how she does it, but she does.

However, it still takes the whole hour of my anatomy class to continue to convince myself that I need to go. I shouldn't let my academic and dance performance start slacking just because I broke up with my boyfriend. I won't let myself stoop to such a pathetic level.

It still sucks though, when I walk out of the locker room dressed in my dance clothes and I see Andrew by the wall having a conversation with Brian. It hurts so bad to see him that I consider just running out of the studio and going back to my dorm and crying my eyes out into my pillow right now. I don't do that though, I just swallow the pain and promise myself that when practice is over, the first thing I have to do is suffocate myself in my pillow and tears. Just two more hours and then I'll be free to cry in private. Hold it out until then and I'll be fine.

"You okay?" Anthony approaches me from behind and puts a hand on my shoulder.

I shrug. "Not really."

"Don't let him get to you, Stell," He tells me. "You'll be fine."

"Yeah, I know that I will be fine, but I am not fine right now," I explain with a shaky breath.

Just as Andrew looks up and we make eye contact, Mr. Lynch announces that we're going to start class so I look away and get into position, standing and facing the front of the classroom as I wait, along with the rest of the class, for Lynch to give us the signal to start stretches.

I notice that Charlotte happily prances into the spot right beside me, glances in my direction with an evil "I won" smirk, and then looks ahead again at our instructor.

I want to tear her to shreds, but I remain still with my face looking straight ahead as if I don't even notice her. I remind myself that it's not her fault that me and Andrew broke up. It was so much more than just Charlotte, but I still hate her because it was like Charlotte was the last straw. Maybe if she wasn't such an imposing bitch, we could have come back from the ledge, stayed a couple, gotten through this rough path.

Mr. Lynch finds somebody to start stretches, and so we stretch and I wonder if Charlotte can feel the hatred I feel towards her radiating off of my body like an aura.

After stretches are done, we all start getting in place to start practice when Charlotte turns to me and grins a wide grin that I want to slap off of her smug European face. "I'm sorry about you and Andrew. Honestly, I am."

I roll my eyes at her but I'm afraid of saying anything back because I'm afraid that if we start arguing, I'm actually going to punch her and then I'd get in trouble and I know for a fact that she'd just let me beat her up just so that I'd get in even more trouble and people would victimize her. I'm smarter than doing that to myself, so I walk away.

About halfway through dance practice, I'm counting in my head like I usually do. "1 2 3 4 5 6 7 8" because that's how it goes and with each number, there's a beat and with each beat, there's a dance move. Putting a number with the position is how I remember the dances. However, I notice myself feeling a sense of being overwhelmed, like I'm suddenly being suffocated by a pillow. The people behind the pillow are probably Andrew and Charlotte and Anthony and my parents and everybody else that's putting pressure on me in some way or another. It's suffocating all at once and then I begin to feel dizzy. I'm dizzy and all I can think about is how Andrew is not my boyfriend anymore. I think about all of the memories that we share and how it is all over. The only memories I have of being his girlfriend are over, there are no more to be made. We are over. There is no more us to be made. I become even dizzier and then my body feels kind of numb and then I see somebody bump into my right side but because my body is so numb, I don't feel it, I just see it happen and then, so that I don't fall down, I bend down and put my hands on my knees and tell myself over and over again,

Please, God, don't throw up. Don't throw up. Please, I am seriously begging you not to throw up right now.

And then, I see a blurry version of Brian running up to me and he's saying something but it's quiet and echoing, as if he's at the end of a long tunnel, shouting at me, and I can't understand what he's saying. I can hear Mr. Lynch calling something out frantically, but again, he's at the end of that tunnel and I can't hear what he's saying. And then, next to Brian, Anthony is there and I can see his lips moving and I can make out what he's saying.

"Are you okay?" He asks me through the tunnel. "Stella, what's wrong?"

And all I can think is,

Please don't throw up. Whatever you do, do not throw up.

And then the second worst thing that could happen, it happens. Luckily, I don't throw up in front of my whole class. Unluckily, my body goes limp and I pass out.

"So you don't know why she just randomly passed out?" I hear somebody's voice near my head.

"It was probably a mix of exhaustion and dehydration," I hear one of the nurses from the clinic speaking. "Overexertion could have had a part in it as well."

"Well, she can still go to practice and everything, right?" I finally place that voice as Brian's and I wonder why he's with me instead of Anthony or Andrew, and then I remember for about the fifteenth time in the past twenty-four hours that we broke up and it hits me like a brick wall over and over.

"Not tomorrow. No classes at all, she needs to be in bed. Not because of the dehydration or anything, but the fall that she took hit her head pretty hard. It's a good thing that thanksgiving break is coming up because if it wasn't, she'd be missing out on about a week of practice. However, I'd say that she'll be good to go when she gets back from break," The nurse explains to him.

I decide to open my eyes now because I'm tired of just laying here, so I open them and then I slowly sit up on the small nurse's bed that I'm lying on.

"Whoa, hey, Stell," Brian greets me as he helps me sit up and steady myself. "How are you feeling?"

"Like I got hit in the head with a brick," I decide with a groan.

"Close. You got hit in the head with a linoleum floor," He corrects me. "Well, the floor got hit by you, but I'm sure there's no difference to you right now."

"Not really," I mumble. "Can I go back to my dorm now?"

"Let me just give you a pill for the headache," The nurse who, now that I can see her, I recognize as Nurse Kenzie, who is in medical school right now and works here with the main nurses on Mondays Wednesdays and Fridays as part of her internship or something like that. She's one of the very few interns we have during the actual school year, actually. She hands me a large white pill that resembles chalk, and then a small Pixie cup of water. I throw the pill into the back of my throat and then take the shot of water as if it was vodka to make swallowing the pill easier, and then it's down my throat.

"Awesome. Thanks a lot for your help, now I can go?" I wonder, just wanting to get back to my room and either sleep or cry but I'll probably end up doing both by crying myself to sleep.

"Yes, you can go," She confirms. "I'll call you both out of the rest of class."

"Wait, class isn't over? How long have I been out of it?" I wonder curiously.

"Only about twenty minutes," Brian supplies as he wraps an arm around my waist to help me off of the uncomfortable bed and onto my feet. I'm a little bit wobbly at first but I quickly get my bearings again and I'm fine. I notice that Brian has my gym bag over his shoulder and his own gym bag in his hand which means that I don't have to go back to the studio to get my clothes or anything and Brian is an awesome friend.

We walk across campus together at a slow pace considering I'm still half awake and suffering from a major headache.

"So An... Um, Anthony is really worried about you," Brian stumbles. I know that he was about to say Andrew but decided that he probably shouldn't, which was a good idea but it's too late now because I already knew what he was going to say.

"You talk to my brother?" I play dumb for a moment before continuing on. "Well, you can tell Anthony that I'm just fine."

"Are you sure that you're just fine?" He wonders skeptically.

"I'm as good as I can be right at this moment," I inform him. "Except for the fact that my head feels like crap and, you know, I feel like my insides are all twisted up wrong and my whole world is spinning way too fast for me to comprehend anymore. And no, it is not because of my period. Okay so no, I'm not as good as I can be right at this moment. But that's normal, isn't it? To feel like this after a breakup like this one? It'll get better. It doesn't feel like it now, but the heartbreak and the world-stopping pain, it'll all go away eventually. It all ends. That's what everybody's saying."

"Wow. You're like your own therapist," Brian tires to joke, but I'm not in the mood to joke at all, and after I don't even attempt to laugh, he clears his throat and frowns. We walk into the dorm building and cross the lobby towards the elevators.

"It does end. Right?" I wonder. "Because it's like the world is moving too fast but it's also not moving at all. And every time I blink, I miss him even more. And my head feels like it's exploding but I think that's just because of that floor punching me in the face."

We go into the elevator and I lean heavily onto the wall so that I don't have to stand on my own because my whole body just feels so heavy right now.

"Do you need some help getting to your room?" Brian wonders, not waiting for my answer before he wraps an arm under my arms to hold some of my weight for me. I think the pill the nurse gave me is setting in now because I'm feeling even more exhausted than I was a little bit ago.

"Thanks, Brian," I sigh tiredly as we walk out of the elevator and down the hallway towards my room. When we get there, Brian pulls my key chain out of my gym bag and unlocks the door.

"Sure. I'll stay with you until you get to sleep," He assures me as we walk in and I stumble my way over to the cozy warm bed.

"Okay. Oh, and by the way, if you ever put Mason through this kind of shit, I will be very mean to you," I inform my friend in all seriousness. Mason is such an innocent, sweet girl. I don't know what I'd do if I had to see her this miserable. I wouldn't be able to take it, that's for sure.

"I know," He chuckles and then I'm closing my eyes and almost instantaneously, I'm asleep and everything goes black.

I will be updating pretty frequently now since I just finished the story- it's only 24 chapters- so that's something <3

8 Tennessee

"I hate snow," I mumble in irritation as I'm walking through about an inch of snow with my tan boots that aren't really boots because they only cover up to my ankle. "How did I let you talk me into this?"

Anthony chuckles from beside me, his teeth chattering almost as badly as mine are, "I didn't talk you into it, Stell, I just asked you if you wanted to come and you said yes. I didn't even know that it snowed in Tennessee."

"I wouldn't have said yes if I knew that there was going to be snow," I mumble in freezing irritation. I mean, it's November so I knew that it was going to be cold so it's not like I'm not dressed for the freezing weather. Since I wasn't allowed to go to school yesterday, I slept late and then went shopping but I was only gone for about an hour, so nobody really noticed that I was gone. It has been years since I've dealt with cold weather though, so I had to get a winter coat and a cute sweater before arriving here in freezing Tennessee for this stupid Thanksgiving vacation.

Not only was it snowing, but we had to walk from the driveway of our grandparents' house to the front door and it's actually a surprisingly long walk. They're very rich, my maternal grandparents are, and they live on this huge piece of land with a huge house and they have a huge staff from butlers to valet to cooks and pool boys (even right now because they have an indoor pool) and they have enough bedrooms to accommodate the whole family, which is why we are all gathering here for the Thanksgiving holiday.

My grandparents had five kids including my mother: Uncle Denny, Aunt Jackie, Aunt Georgie, and Aunt Theresa. Denny and his wife had two kids of their own- Michael, who is 32, and Sarah, who is 29. Michael and his wife have two little kids (Timmy-5 and Ericka-2) and Sarah is pregnant with her first child. Jackie married and she now has four grown up kids. Emily is 25 and engaged, Harry is 23 and has a newborn baby with his girlfriend named Jayda, Riley and Jamie are 19 year old twins. Georgie and her husband only had one kid- TJ, who is 27. Theresa never married but she adopted two kids from China a while ago- Brian, who is now 13, and Miracle (we all just call her Mary), who is now 10.

Basically, there's a little over thirty people that will be staying in this one house, that's how big it is. I honestly haven't seen any of these people since I left for Vaughn and I don't think Anthony has either, so we spent our whole flight from LA to Tennessee looking through Facebook and printed photo albums as we remembered everybody and their names and faces and got caught up with who had kids, who's about to have kids, and who got married or is about to do so.

"Okay, so from what I remember, we are the sanest people from this family," I start as we get closer to the front door. "So if we split up and then get bombarded by a family member or members and their craziness, we need a code word so that the other person will come in and save the other."

"Oh, God, the twins," Anthony recalls how the twins, who are only a year older than us, feel like just because they are twins and Anthony and I are twins that all four of us share some weird connection. They're also really into science and the brain, so they always ask us to do experiments and it's really creepy and weird. "Yeah, we'll definitely need a safe word."

"Okay, so how about... Pecan," I suggest. "If you hear me say that, you need to hightail your ass over to me and I'll do the same for you. This family is crazy. We need to stick together in there."

He nods in agreement as we walk up to the front door. Because we are only going to be here for a few days, I just washed out my gym bag and stuffed all of my clothes in that so that I didn't have to bring a real suitcase, which is what Anthony did too, so I clutch my stuffed gym bag over my shoulder as Anthony knocks on the door.

Almost immediately, the door swings open and a man dressed in a fancy tuxedo is standing there. I don't recognize him as part of the family, so I'm assuming that he's one of the butlers.

"Welcome to the Claymont Estate!" He grins at us eagerly. "May I take your bags?"

"Uh. Sure?" I mutter as we both hand the man our gym bags.

"Great, I take it that you two are Stella and Anthony?" He asks us and when we both nod, his grin widens.

I impatiently step through the door, tired of standing on the porch while I freeze my butt off so as I push politely past the butler, Anthony follows my lead and follows me in as we're immediately drown in a feeling of warmth from the nice heating system in this huge mansion of a house.

"My name is Bart and Greta here will take your coats," He announces, motioning towards an older lady that's dressed in black pants and a white blouse so she's either a maid or a female butler (Do those even exist? I guess they probably do since it's the twenty-first century or maybe that's just the same as a maid).

Both me and Anthony slide our heavy winter coats off and hand them to Greta, who takes them somewhere out of sight and Bart starts to lead us up the grand flight of stairs.

"I will take you two to your room. The rest of the family has already arrived and they are enjoying their afternoon on the mountain skiing. Would you like to join them?"

"No," I say quickly, loving the fact that I get today to prepare for tomorrow, which is Thanksgiving, so it'll be the big family oriented day of mingling and hearing everybody complain about the fact that I watch what I eat. "I feel rather jetlagged, so I think I'm just going to take a nap."

"Yeah, I don't want to go skiing either," Anthony shakes his head as we follow Bart down a few hallways decorated like a freaking Elizabethan castle or something until we finally reach the door.

"Here is your room. Are you two okay with sharing a room?" Bart wonders as he opens the door and glides in. We both follow him and I realize how big the bedroom is with a huge dresser, two twin sized beds on both the right and left walls, and a huge TV with a couch and a coffee table. It reminds me of the Mia's bedroom in The Princess Diaries.

"That's fine," Anthony comments. Bart puts both of our bags down near the door and then smiles back up at us.

"You'll find a full map of the estate on both nightstands. Feel free to explore and look around with your free time today. Tomorrow, breakfast is at eight A.M. in the grand dining room and you won't have much free time tomorrow, so get all of your exploring done today. It really is a magnificent place, I suggest you take advantage of the experience."

"Eight A.M.?" I wonder incredulously. "Can we just skip breakfast if we just want to sleep?"

"Mrs. Claymont is eager to start the day," Bart explains. "She insists that everyone attend all of the Thanksgiving events that she and Mr. Claymont have planned out. Are there any more questions?"

"Do we get dinner tonight?" Anthony wonders.

"Dinner will be delivered to your room at seven tonight," Bart tells us.

"Okay thanks, I think we can take it from here," I say, eager to get the butler out of the room so that we can just relax for a while before we get hit with a whole lot of crazy. Including our parents, who aren't as crazy as the twins but they're still intolerable for a long period of time.

The butler nods. "If you need anything, please call the extension that is printed on the map," He tells us before scurrying out of the room and shutting the door behind him.

I quickly lock the door and then I turn to face Anthony. "This was a big mistake."

"I'm realizing that," He sighs, sitting down on the twin bed that's on the right side of the room.

"How can they expect me to be able to deal with all of their crazy at eight in the morning? I can barely handle my own crazy that early in the morning."

"It'll be fine, Stell, it's just for a few days," Anthony assures me as I sit down on the other bed and then I lay down and tell myself to calm down. Anthony's right. It's just a few days and then we're back to the real world. But is that really comforting right now? The real world? Where I have to deal with Charlotte and Andrew.

Maybe I'm not really freaking out about being here, stuck in Elizabethan Limbo, I'm just afraid that the real world that's waiting for me back in LA is no better. Maybe even worse. The craziness of my family still can't drown out the black hole that is swallowing my insides and it gets bigger every day, every hour, every minute. I miss him. I can't stop thinking about him, even as I'm being forced into this crazy house with crazy people.

"Hey," Anthony interrupts my train of thought. "Stop thinking about him, okay? This is a vacation- as fucked up as it may be- so just try your best to enjoy yourself without thinking about anything from back home."

"That's a lot easier said than done," I mumble as I lift my heavy head from the comfortable pillows and grab the map from the nightstand. "I think I'm going to go find that pool."

"That's the spirit," He assures me with a small, encouraging smile. "I think I'm going to the game room. I don't know why our grandparents have a game room, but hopefully it's entertaining."

"Why do they need 99% of the stuff that they have here?" I wonder. "They don't need any of it, they just have it for no reason at all."

"True," He agrees.

I pull my bikini out of my bag and go into the bathroom that's attached to our room to get dressed and then slip on my sweater over top of the bikini so that I'm somewhat covered up as I walk through the house to find the pool. I grab the map in hopes that it will help me not get lost and then I say goodbye to Anthony and tell him to text me in case of emergency because I have my phone with me.

In the hallways, I pass two butlers and a maid (female butler?) that just wave as I walk by but luckily, I don't run into any family members. I think they're all still on the mountain skiing like Bart said and I sincerely hope that they're gone for a while. I'm pretty sure that those creepy twins are going to hunt me and Anthony down once they find out that we're here so I'd like to procrastinate that event from happening for as long as possible.

I find the pool pretty easily on the first floor and as I walk into the humid area, I hear loud-ish music playing and there's a guy standing on the edge of the pool on the other side with one of those pool cleaning things on the long stick. I'm about to ask him if the pool is closed or something, but when he hears the door close behind me, he looks up abruptly and then curses as he shuts off the music.

"I'm so sorry, Ma'am, I thought that everybody went skiing."

"Um, why are you sorry?" I ask the guy in confusion.

"Well, the music and everything," He explains. "I didn't know anybody was home."

"I just got here," I explain. "For the family thing. Is it okay if I hang out in here?"

"Yeah, of course," He nods so I walk into the room and walk over to one of the lounge chairs, putting my phone down on the plastic table beside it before sitting down on the chair. "Let me just pack up and I'll be out of here."

"You don't have to leave," I say quickly, realizing now that this is probably one of their pool boys. "I mean, it'd be stupid for you to leave just because I'm here. I don't mind."

"Really?" He wonders. "Are you sure?"

I nod and lay back on the chair as if I was under the sun getting a tan. Obviously, though, we're indoors and if we were outside, I'd more likely get frostbite instead of a tan. Laying back like this by the pool is still a little bit relaxing, I guess. "Yeah. I don't mind some company. I'm Stella."

"Uh, Jeremy," He informs me. "And you're a Claymont?"

I nod and look up at the ceiling as I try not to miss him, I try to stay engaged in this conversation with the pool boy and not think of Andrew at all, but it's so hard. I feel so empty inside and not thinking about Andrew is as impossible as not breathing yet continuing to live. "Unfortunately. And you're the pool boy?"

"Unfortunately," He confirms my suspicions. "It's getting me through college though, so I guess it's worth it."

"Do they even ever use the pool?" I ask him curiously.

"Not at all," He laughs. "But they still pay me way too much money to clean it twice a week."

"So how do you deal with snow?" I ask him. "I mean, I used to have to live with it a lot because I'm from Maine, but I go to school in LA now and I completely hate it. When I go to college though, I'm going to have to deal with it again and I just don't know if I'm up for that."

"Where are you going to college?" He wonders.

"Julliard," I supply, continuing to look at the ceiling while I continue to try to not think of Andrew but the harder I try not to, the harder it is to ignore his presence in my mind. I miss him so much and it hasn't even been a week since we broke up.

"Wow, really? For what?" Jeremy asks me from the other side of the pool as he continues to clean around the sides.

"Dance," I mutter.

"Isn't it like, really hard to get into that school though?"

I nod and then I begin to brag in the most subtle way that I can muster, but that's still not very subtle because I'm not a subtle person. "It is. I already got accepted though. Full ride scholarship and everything."

"Wow," He says again, obviously impressed, which used to give me a sense of pride. Hearing people get all impressed when I told them about my accomplishments that are pretty major and brag-worthy, but that sense of pride was taken away from me when this black hole started to swirl inside of me. It doesn't matter anymore. I feel so empty. I miss him. "Congratulations."

"Thanks," I sigh, standing up from the chair. "So the pool's clean, right? Like, I can go swimming in it?"

"Yeah, it's clean," He assures me.

"Awesome," I mumble, slipping my crème sweater with an owl on the front off of me and I toss it into the lounge chair that I was just sitting on. I'm feeling agitated, like I'm a smoker who needs a cigarette. Only I'm just a pathetic heartbroken girl who needs an Andrew. But since I can't have him, I need to cry. Crying is like my nicotine patch for getting over my Andrew Addiction although, it isn't working too well, it just makes me hurt even more but I still can't stop. I haven't cried since this morning though, and it's going to start coming out soon. Hopefully, I can swim for a little while before I'm overwhelmed with a since of hopeless need for my ex-boyfriend who, at the moment, is spending his time with his family in New Mexico, where there is no snow.

With a running start, I dive into the deep end of the pool and swim underwater until my lungs feel like they're going to explode. I then resurface and let out a long breath. And then I go underwater again and I hold my breath until my lungs feel like they're on fire, burning inside of my chest and then I hold on some more. I only resurface when I feel like I might pass out soon. Underwater, everything is silent. Peaceful. It's a feeling that I desperately need right now. Gasping for breath, I start to swim from one end of the pool to the other for a while in hopes that if I keep moving, I can keep thoughts of Andrew at bay, but it doesn't work for long. Soon,

I'm a trembling mess as I try as hard as I can not to think of Andrew but I can never stop.

Eventually, when I resign to my fate, I swim to the edge of the pool and pull myself up to sit on the edge and I lay back on the hard surface behind me, press my face into my hands and then I begin to softly cry. The mix of chlorine and salty tears burn my eyes so I try to wipe them away with my palm but it doesn't help that much.

"Hey, are you okay?" I hear Jeremy ask me.

I nod as I'm trying to get myself to stop crying. "Yeah," I sniffle. "Just a little bit emotionally unstable right now."

As I'm standing up to my feet, I remember how I spent the beginning of my summer hooking up with this guy named Drew. We weren't dating but we'd have casual sex maybe once a week or so and I thought that it made my problems go away a little bit. The idea that sex will make my problems go away is completely idiotic and ridiculous and I know that, but it still crosses my mind that maybe I could sleep with this Jeremy guy. It's only a fleeting idea before it's gone again but just the fact that I even thought about it in the first place makes me start crying again. I sit down where I was sitting before, careful not to get my sweater wet, and put my face back in my hands. My shoulders quake with sobs as I start to cry even harder than before. I miss him.

"Here, maybe this will help?" Jeremy awkwardly offers me a large white towel. I take it and bury my face into the softness of the towel in hopes of muffling some of my embarrassing cries.

"I'm sorry," I mumble after a minute as Jeremy is continuing to clean the pool but he's still watching me with a concerned gaze. "I'm probably really annoying right now."

"It's fine," He assures me. "You don't have to apologize for crying."

"It's just that I almost wanted to sleep with you," I tell him although I'm sure he doesn't want to hear my life story, I just start talking as if that will help the pain go away. I know that it's not true though. I know that nothing will make this pain go away, no matter what I try. "And that makes me so sad."

"Erm. I'm sorry?" He obviously wasn't expecting my level of raw honesty. I'm not used to being around people that aren't used to my incredible bluntness so I should probably work on keeping things to myself. At least while I'm here in Tennessee. "That does sound pretty tragic."

"No, I mean it's just that the last time that I had casual sex with somebody, I was in such a dark place and I just... I don't want to go back to that dark place, you know? And I'd also probably start crying halfway through so that'd be a major turn off. And I'm sorry that I talk too much. I know that I talk too much, my friends in LA just know how to deal with it. This is such a disaster. I'm going to go back to my room now," I finally decide as I blubber my way through an embarrassing apology. I dry my face for the last time and then grab my phone and my sweater. I hiccup once and then sniffle but other than that, I'm as good as new. I'm going to hold in the rest of my crying until I'm back in my room and I'll take a shower to drown out the sounds.

"Are you sure that you're okay?" He wonders. "I can walk you to your room or something?"

"I'm fine," I mutter. "Thank you though. Bad breakups are... you know, bad and everything. Thanks again, Jeremy. It was nice talking to you."

"Sure. I'll see you tomorrow, Stella," He tells me.

"You will?" I question.

He nods. "Yeah, I'll be serving food. I don't usually do that sort of stuff but they asked and it's just some extra cash."

"But don't you have your own family to spend Thanksgiving with?" I ask him.

"My family lives in Connecticut and I couldn't afford to fly up there, so I'm just going to work," He explains.

"Oh. Well I'll see you tomorrow then," I mumble, too embarrassed to stay and talk with him anymore so I just turn and hurry out of the room and follow the map so that I can get back to the grand staircase and up to my room. I'm grateful that he gave me that towel because I wasn't going to put my sweater back on and get it wet so at least I can walk through the house at least slightly covered up.

Anthony isn't in the room when I get there so I hop into the shower and I spend way too much time in there because I decide that the shower, where nobody can interrupt me or hear me, is the best place to cry. The black hole inside of me has sucked out my ability to feel emotions except for sadness and loneliness because those are really the only two things that I've been able to feel lately and it's so exhausting to be sad all of the time but there's nothing that I can do about that, like I've said. I miss him so much and it's only been four days. How can I live like this? With my chest burning with an empty vacancy all of the time? How can this get easier? I doubt that it ever will.

Out of the shower, I get dressed in sweat pants and a loose long sleeved t-shirt and, before I leave the bathroom, I rub on some foundation in an attempt to hide the fact that I'd been crying from Anthony when he returns to the room from the game room.

It's still early so if I wanted to, I'm sure that I could still go explore this mansion but I honestly don't feel like it anymore. The whole place is crawling with butlers and maids as they prepare for the hell that is tomorrow and I don't feel like talking to people. I also want to be in the safety of this room when everybody comes back from skiing- I didn't even know that people skied in Tennessee. Are there even mountains here?- so that I don't get bombarded by creepy questions from the twins or my parents, pretending like they've missed us. It has been a while since they've seen us but I know that they could care less about seeing me and Anthony. We shouldn't have even come.

I almost pick up the phone to call Mason but then I realize that she's spending tonight with Brian since both of their families live near campus, they stay in the dorms but not a lot of people do, so they enjoy the time that they have in solitude and run around campus and be all coupley and stuff so I don't want to interrupt their time together. Sienna's family lives near campus too, but she's spending the break with her boyfriend at his parents' house since he has Thanksgiving break right now too and they don't want to stay in Penn's dorm for the rest of the week. I think Sienna said something about Penn's parents being away anyway, so they have the house almost to themselves- Penn's sister is still there but it still must be nice. If Andrew and I were still together and we weren't fighting like we had been, I would have gone to New Mexico with him to see his family. We'd already talked about it and planned it and everything but then… you know, things changed. I wonder if he's going to tell them that we broke up when they ask about me.

I wonder if I'm going to tell my family that we broke up if they ask about him.

I'm sitting on the couch watching reruns of Friends when Anthony shows up in the room a few hours later.

"Lock the door," I remind him as he shuts the door behind him. He turns and locks the door before coming over to the couch and sitting down beside me. "How was the game room?"

"It was actually really impressive," He tells me. "They have a bunch of arcade games that I haven't played since I was like, ten. How was the pool?"

"It was nice," I mutter, running my fingers through my hair absentmindedly. "I met the pool boy. He was pretty cool."

"Do you think that you're ready for tomorrow?"

I shrug. "I'm as ready as I'll ever be. But really, can you ever be ready to deal with these people?"

"Okay, that's a good point," He agrees. "Do you think that they'll bring up our... erm, falling out?"

"Do you think that they know about our falling out?" I ask him with raised eyebrows. "I highly doubt that Mom would admit to her family that her kids aren't as perfect as they had originally thought."

"God, I hope you're right. Can you imagine the field day that the twins would have if they found out about it?" Anthony wonders with a small groan.

"Oh my, God, I didn't even think about that," I laugh as I try to imagine the types of questions they would ask us. "'Were you physically ill when you were fighting with Anthony?' I really hope that I'm right about Mom keeping that a secret. I don't feel like explaining it to them anyway."

"Should we run over the names again?" He suggests.

I nod and then I go get my laptop and Anthony is holding the photo album book thing that has all of the family members and their names written below their pictures.

"Hey," I nudge my brother with my shoulder after a while of going over the family and putting names with faces, "I know that we've had our differences but these people really have no boundaries. We have to stick together tomorrow. No matter what. Okay?"

"Yeah, I know," Anthony assures me. "We'll stick together."

"I'm going to go to bed early," I inform him as I stand up from the couch and hand him the remote after we put up the album and the laptop, calling it a night with the faces and names. Whatever we forget now, we forget and there's no stopping it. We tried the best that we could.

"Goodnight, Stell," He sighs, changing the channel as I walk across the room and crawl into bed. However, even with the lights off, I find it pretty difficult to find sleep, so I listen to what Anthony is watching, which is Family Guy and then American Dad. I have my eyes closed and my face stuffed into the pillow so I just listen and hope that I'll be able to get to sleep but even as midnight rolls around and Anthony decides to go to sleep, I'm still awake, not even on the brink of sleep.

I watch Netflix for another hour, until it's one, and then I decide that I need to get to sleep or I'll be exhausted tomorrow even more so than I already am day by day. I try to go to sleep in the pitch black of the room, the only sounds are Anthony's soft snores from across the room (luckily, he's not a loud snorer). However, it's suddenly two A.M. and all I can think about is Andrew and all of the memories that we had together. It occurs to me that it's 2 A.M. and I'm sitting here, feeling my heart break for him when he's probably sound asleep across the country.

9 Thanksgiving-1

Every morning, for just about two seconds just as I wake up, I forget about reality. I look over and expect to see Andrew laying there next to me but when my arm reaches over into empty space, I panic and look to see that he's not there. And then I remember. Like a tidal wave, it all comes crashing down on me again and I remember.

"Stella," Anthony says, just as I'm getting over the initial panic of waking up. "Are you okay?"

"I'm fine," I breathe, plopping back down onto my back and looking up at the ceiling. It's like losing him all over again every single morning and it's excruciating. I wonder if this will ever go away but I doubt it. "How much time to we have until breakfast?"

"Half an hour," He tells me.

I sit up and remind myself that I'm about to spend about twelve hours with my crazy family. I cannot afford to be sad over Andrew right now. Unfortunately, there's no switch inside of my brain that can turn off my emotions or my sadness. "Awesome," I breathe sarcastically.

"It's just one day," Anthony tells me with a forced yet encouraging smile as he walks away and starts to fish through his duffel bag to fish out his outfit for today.

"Yeah, just one day," I mumble tiredly as I stand up and get my own outfit out- a dark red chiffon dress with long sheer sleeves, black underwear and black pantyhose since the dress is kind of short, I figure the hose will cover my legs up more. I hop into the shower for only about ten minutes and then I get out, dry my hair and everything and then get dressed before washing my face and then applying silver-blackish eye makeup and some lip gloss. My hair dries in its natural waves and I decide not to mess with it except with a little bit of product. It's my crazy family, not the president of the United States, I don't really have anybody to impress.

"At least we get food," Anthony adds as I walk out of the bathroom and start to poke my gold hoop earrings through my ears. "I mean, they hired a huge array of chefs and everything so the food has to be amazing, right?"

"Yeah, well while you're pigging out on a million dollar pancake, I'm going to get an earful of them complaining about me watching what I eat. Seriously, I don't think that any of them- especially Mom- understands the concept of keeping myself healthy."

"Okay, that's true," He concedes, buttoning up his blue button up dress shirt. Fortunately, we didn't accidently match our outfits because the last time we had a family gathering- I believe it was the Christmas before we moved to Vaughn- I wore a red and silver dress and Anthony wore a red dress shirt so it looked like we matched but we didn't do it on purpose- it was Christmas, everyone was wearing red. However, the twins disagreed and they continuously yapped about how twins unintentionally match their clothes all of the time because of some neurological resemblance.

We have five minutes to get downstairs for breakfast as I'm slipping my tan pumps onto my feet. "Let's do this thing. I pray that nothing goes disastrous," And by disastrous, I mean that I hope that they don't bring up Andrew. I know that my parents know about him because I told them about him but I don't know if they told the rest of the family or not. I don't even know if they would remember something like that, but I really hope that they didn't. Or at least they just decide not to ask about him.

"Remember- we stick together," I remind my brother just as he finishes tucking his shirt into his black dress pants and we stand by the door, readying ourselves for the last time before we begin the day. "And the SOS is pecan."

"Right," He nods. "Pecan."

"Wait, we should change it. What if they have pecan pie? I love pecan pie but you might think it's the signal," I explain. "Let's change it to mermaid."

"Okay then," Anthony laughs a little bit. "Mermaid is the signal then. Are you ready?"

I nod with a deep breath. "Yeah. Let's go."

And so we go. We follow the map to the grand dining room (on the map, it's called a dining hall though, that's how big it is). It takes us downstairs and through the grand foyer to the other side of the house and when we get close enough, we can hear the clink of dishes and the mumbling of friendly chatter.

I give Anthony one last look of apprehensiveness and he returns the look before we step into the doorway where everyone can see us. Here we go. The dining table is long and the plates are already set, there's just no food on them yet, and they look really fancy. White plates with a gold ribbon rolling around the outer edges and matching mugs. The table looks almost full, so I guess we are the last people to show up and that's probably because we are the most un-eager people here.

"Stella!" I hear a high pitched squeal just as another high pitched squeal yelps "Anthony!" and before I even realize what's happening, we're being bombarded by two nerdy looking nineteen year old girls. The twins. Riley and Jamie but I don't know who's who. They pride themselves on being absolutely identical in every phrase of the word, so it's impossible to tell which one is which. They have different colored eyes but one of them wears colored contacts so that you can't tell. They both have frizzy dirty blonde hair and thick rimmed glasses with pointy noses and crooked yet strangely pretty smiles. Right now, they're wearing a black maxi dress and a clunky crème cardigan with matching crème flats. Even though they're a year older than me, I tower over them in my heels. The one that's hugging me tightly against her is barely taller than my nose.

"Oh, hi," I clear my throat and force myself to sound polite. "It's been a while."

"A while?" Thing 1 wonders incredulously and then cackles with laughter.

"It's been four years!" Thing 2 exclaims, matching her sister's cackling as they finally release me and my brother. "You got so…"

"Tall," Thank 1 finishes. "Both of you."

"Yes," Thing 2 continues. "You both have remarkable growth rates."

"Well, like you said, it's been four years. And I'm wearing heels," I explain.

"Come sit with us," Thing 1 tells us as she grabs my hand and the other one grabs Anthony's hand and they start dragging us to the other end of the table where they are sitting. They sit on one side and they motion for us to sit in the two seats across from them.

"We saved them for you," Thing 2 explains but I notice that Anthony doesn't sit down and so I don't either.

"That's really nice of you guys," He tells them. "We'll be right back though, we should go say hi to our parents."

"Yes," I sigh, excited to have a little excuse to prolong the time between now and having to sit down with the twins, which we obviously have to do because there's no way to get out of sitting with them while not being rude as well.

We find our parents sitting in the middle of the table in a tense conversation with my uncle about the stock so neither one of them notice us walk up behind them.

To get their attention, I tap on my mother's shoulder so she turns around and when she sees us, she grins.

"Oh, lovely!" She exclaims, standing up from the table to greet us. My dad notices us as well and then stands to join our mom. "Hello, darlings."

"Hi, Mom," I smile at her. I know that they are cold people- they aren't bad or villainous, they just lack the emotions that usually come with being parents- and they aren't particularly involved in our lives like parents should be, but they are still my parents and I still miss them since I only ever see them maybe once every few months or so.

She doesn't make a move to hug either one of us though, and I don't expect her to. She just puts a hand on my shoulder, which is basically her version of a hug and my dad shakes Anthony's hand, which is his version of a hug. "It's so nice to see you. How have you been?" My mom asks us.

"Busy," Anthony answers. "With school and everything."

"Good grades and everything, I hope?" My dad wonders. When he was fresh out of college, my dad started a company with a few friends and it immediately took off and then he met my mom and they got married here in Tennessee. When they wanted to expand the company, my dad was elected to be the one to move up to Maine to open another plant (I'm not entirely sure what this company was) and so he and my mom moved up there right after the wedding and that's when she got pregnant with us. For the next fourteen years, we all lived in Maine but because my dad was always working and flying between Maine and Tennessee, we never saw him. When my mother wasn't flying with my dad to Tennessee (they wouldn't take us because it'd interfere with school), she'd be away at the country club with her friends so we'd never see her either. She didn't have a job because between our father's company and her family's inherited money, we were already billionaires. When it was time for Anthony and I to go to high school, they shipped us off to Vaughn where we easily got in (we were taking dance lessons since we could walk because our first nanny was a dancer and we thought it was so cool). They sold the house in Maine, my dad sold his share of the company, and they bought an RV and started traveling around the continental U.S. without a care in the world.

"Yeah, good grades," I confirm. "How's the RV and everything?"

"Oh, it's marvelous. We're thinking about going up to Alaska this spring and it'll be really beautiful," My mom explains. "It's too bad that you guys will be too busy with school to come with us."

"Too bad," Anthony agrees with them just like we do every time that they do that, because they do it a lot. 'We're going to this marvelous place. Too bad that you can't go'.

"Well, we're going to sit down for breakfast so we'll catch up some more later," My dad tells us before giving me one of his business like handshakes and my mother squeezes Anthony's shoulder- the closest thing to affection that we receive from them at all- and then we return to sitting across from the twins.

A few waiters enter the room with plates of food which confuses me because we already have plates so I don't understand how that's going to work. When the first waiters stop at the other end of the table, I find out that the first plate is just a place mat for the actual plate with food on it that looks identical to the white and gold plates we have already. They place the plate with food on it on top of the empty plate with a quiet 'clink' and the waiters continue to spill out of the kitchen door until all of us have a food full of breakfast foods. Pancakes, hash browns, bacon, eggs, biscuits, and a side bowl of gravy. Seriously, who eats this much?

I look around the large group of suit-wearing waiters and look for Jeremy's face. I see him and when he notices me staring at him, we make eye contact and he winks at me. I smile back at him, too afraid to wave because somebody might notice it and then I'd get a lecture for fraternizing with "the help".

"Please enjoy your breakfast," One of the waiters said. "If you need anything, feel free to grab one of us and we will be more than happy to accommodate you."

Some of the waiters left the room but about half of them stayed and stood by the walls, lurking for one of us to need something from them. Jeremy is one of the ones that leave the room, so I don't see him again for a while.

"Okay, so we noticed that you didn't color code your outfits today," Thing 1 begins to speak as she digs into the scrambled eggs. I don't want to eat all of these carbs but if I ask for a healthier option, I'll get a lecture about eating and how I'm "too skinny".

"Yeah, we don't plan our outfits together," Anthony informs them.

"Really? That's fascinating," Thing 2 mumbles with wide eyes. She too, is starting with the scrambled eggs. I wonder if they are eating the same foods at the same time on purpose. It really wouldn't surprise me. "I realize that it would be more difficult to match your clothing given the fact that you are of different sexes though."

"Very good point," Thing 1 agrees as if we're their science project or something, but we just let them go at it because we don't really have another choice.

"Even if we were of the same sex, I don't think we'd dress the same," I tell them although I know that I should keep my mouth shut, it just seems so ridiculous. Sure, dressing the same is cute for twins when they're little, but it drives right into crazy at about thirteen years old and they still match everything- including underwear. "Individuality is really important to me."

"But you're twins," Thing 2 reminds me.

"Yeah, but that doesn't mean that we're the same person," I defend with a small laugh. "We're pretty different people, actually."

"Fascinating," They both say at the same exact time and it's so creepy that it sends chills down my spine as I'm nibbling on one of the biscuits.

"Do you feel a sexual attraction for the same people?" Thing 1 wonders.

"We're both straight," Anthony informs them before I can reply, which is smart, because I would have said something incredibly sarcastic and probably very rude if I were to answer that question. Is that really an appropriate kind of question to ask people? I really don't think so.

"Well, that doesn't really mean anything. You can be straight but still feel aroused by somebody of the same sex," Thing 2 informs us, but I'm not so sure that she's correct. I mean, I don't think that's how sexuality works at all, but I'm not going to argue with them because they're so incredibly stubborn that it would be useless.

"So our question still stands," Thing 1 adds. "Do you share a sexual attraction?"

Anthony looks over at me with a grin and I glare at him, warning him not to say what I know he's about to say. "Stell, did you want to have sex with Gianna?"

I bite back a laugh at the absurdity of the idea and the sarcasm that my brother just emptied into that question, but neither of the twins noticed the sarcasm because they're both looking at me expectantly, waiting for my response. "Strangely enough, I did not. I actually hated her guts."

"Wait, so you, Anthony, had intercourse with a girl that you, Stella, did not get along with?" Thing 2 wonders incredulously.

"That's... horrendous," Thing 1 babbles as if we just told them that the earth is going to end tomorrow by an alien attack from Jupiter. "Did it hurt?"

"Did what hurt?" Anthony wonders in confusion.

"The intercourse," Thing 1 elaborates. "I mean, all of the negative energy that you must have been feeling while having intercourse with this girl must have been physically alarming, am I right?"

"You didn't climax, is that correct?" Thing 2 asks while pushing her glasses up her face. I chose the bad time to take a drink of my orange juice because now, I'm trying hard not to spit it out both from laughing and from shock of that question. The twins don't seem to notice my reaction to the question because they're looking so intently at Anthony, awaiting his response.

"Uh, that's kind of personal," He mumbles before shoving half of a strip of bacon into his mouth.

"It's for science," Thing 1 justifies and Thing 2 is nodding in agreement with her sister. "We have to know."

Anthony looks over to me for help, but I just shrug because I have no idea what to say to get him out of this. It's not like I want to hear my brother talk about this stuff because I really don't, but I just can't think of anything that could get the twins to relent on this subject. Like I said, they're very stubborn.

"Um," Anthony trails off before resigning to his fate. "No. It's not correct. And I didn't think about Stella when I was with my girlfriend at all."

"But that just doesn't make any sense," Thing 1 refutes. "The chemical imbalance must have thrown things off."

"We will have to consult our charts when we get home," Thing 2 announces as they both try to figure out this very awkward puzzle that is floating around in their minds.

"Definitely," Thing 1 agrees. "Anyway, so we are interested in another thing as well. We, both being girls, have the same menstrual cycle."

"Oh, my God," I hear Anthony grumble under his breath as he can see where this is going.

"So what our question is," Thing 2 continues. "Is that since you clearly don't have the same menstrual cycle, are you still able to sense when Stella is on her period? Just an instinct or something."

"Or maybe you cramp up too? Twins can sometimes feel each other's pain," Thing 1 elaborates.

"I'm sure we can feel each other's pain right now," I mutter quietly.

"No, I don't know any of that. I guess we just aren't as connected as you guys are," Anthony explains to the twins. I wonder how long breakfast is going to take because I seriously can't take much longer of this and I know that breakfast just started. After this, though, I hope that we can do something that has nothing to do with sitting at a table with these twins.

"This is just remarkable," Thing 1 mutters. "We need to do a follow up appointment."

"I concur," Thing 2 says. "Are you two available next weekend?"

"We'll be in LA," I remind them quickly, desperate to find the perfect, fool proof excuse to not meet up with these two for at least another year or so. "That's where we go to school."

"Right, but maybe we could meet up somewhere?" They offer. Except for my mom, the rest of the family stayed here in Tennessee so they all live around here in smaller houses within a half an hour driving radius from here and the twins went to a community college to stay close to the family- apparently, my mother was also the only one out of her side of the family to miss the "family matters" gene. "Like, maybe you can fly back here and say hi to the family again."

"You want us to fly across the country again next weekend?" I wonder with raised eyebrows.

They both nod and Thing 1 says, "In the name of science. So you'll do it?"

"We can't," Anthony speaks up. "We have a show coming up right before winter break, so we're going to be pretty busy."

That's not a lie. "He's right. Sorry. Maybe next year. Anyway, how's school? You started college this year, right?" I say, desperate to get the conversation twisted onto them instead of me and Anthony.

"Oh, yes," Thing 1 smiles. "We are studying psychology with a strong focus on the connection between twins."

"Shocker," I breathe so that they can't hear me but Anthony has to hold back a small laugh.

"That's interesting," Anthony lies. "How are your classes going?"

"We like them very much," Thing 2 says. "It's all so fascinating."

"I'm going to go to the bathroom," I say softly, deciding that I need a break- even if it isn't for very long.

I stand up from my seat and push the fancy chair in as I notice the twins staring at Anthony intently.

"What?" He asks them, noticing their staring as well.

"Aren't you going to go with her?" Thing 1 asks him as if that's the completely normal thing to do.

"Why would I do that?" He wonders.

Thing 2 rolls her eyes and then says, "Because you're twins."

"But-" He starts and then clamps his mouth shut again. "Okay, you're right. I'll go with her."

And so we walk down the hallway together and turn another corner so that we're not visible by the family or any of the staff.

"Holy shit," I breathe, leaning my back against the wall. "If I hear the word 'intercourse' one more time, I'm going to lose it."

"If I hear the word 'menstruate' one more time, I'm going to be right there with you," Anthony mumbles. "Seriously, are they even human?"

I let out a small laugh. "They may be robots."

"That would explain so much," He tells me. "I think we can get through this though- breakfast should be over soon so maybe we'll be able to get away from them after that."

"I hope so," I sigh. "If they're still talking to us after breakfast, I'm going to fake some kind of sickness because if I don't, I will actually go insane."

"And I will just have to go with you to make sure that you're okay," Anthony adds. "But we have to try and stick it out for as long as possible. They're insane, but they are family and I think we should at least try to spend some time with them before we blow our brains out."

"I know, you're right," I agree with him with a small sigh. "But seriously, do you think that they go to the bathroom together?"

"I have no idea. They seriously freak me out," He says. "I think they literally do everything together."

"Come on," I say as we start walking in the direction that we came from, back to the breakfast. "I don't want them to come looking for us."

"Yeah, I don't think it's a good idea to be alone with them. I think they might want to dissect us," He jokes just before we join the rest of the group to finish breakfast, which is over pretty soon after we return as the waiters come back and take our plates. Mine is still pretty full because I didn't eat all that much but Anthony's is completely clean.

"Okay everyone," My grandma stands up from where she's sitting at the other end of the table. "Now that we've all eaten and the game is about to begin, the men are going to go into the living room for football and the ladies will follow me for some tea."

"What?" I wonder under my breath, hoping that I'd heard her wrong. Not only were they severely separating me and Anthony, but that means that I'll be alone with the twins. How can I survive being alone with the twins?!

"And after the game, we will meet up for a lovely lunch," She continues with a wide smile and then she starts walking away from the table towards one of the hallways and I notice that all of the females in the room start to follow her. My grandpa, who was sitting next to my grandma, starts walking in the other direction and the guys go in his direction.

"Tony, I can't do this alone," I hiss at him without moving from my spot.

"Hey, it'll be fine," He assures me. "If you need me, just come and get me or something and keep your distance from the twins."

"Yeah," I nod. "It'll be fine."

"It'll be totally fine," He agrees before he starts walking away, following the guys towards the football game as I find my legs pushing me away from my brother- the only person keeping me sane right now- and towards my grandma, my mom, my aunts, and my female cousins.

"So, Brenda, how are the kids?" My grandma wonders, looking expectantly Michael's wife as we are all sitting down in a lounge-like area with a bunch of comfortable chairs circled around a large round coffee table that's topped with a bunch of coasters and empty tea cups. I make it a point to sit down as far away from the twins as I possibly can so that when I sit down, I'm between my Aunt Georgie and little ten year old Mary.

"They're really good," Brenda nods enthusiastically as she's holding her two year old daughter on her lap. I'd never met Ericka, since it's been four years since I've seen any of these people, but she looks a lot like her mother- blonde hair, bright green eyes, and a round nose. She's really cute, the toddler is, and I wish that I could just start playing with her right now because she's probably the only person in this whole room that I am able to get along with for longer than an hour at a time. "Timmy will be starting school next year."

"They're growing up so fast," My mom comments. "Stella and Anthony are graduating high school this year."

"Oh, how exciting!" Aunt Jackie (who spawned the twins) squeals with a wide grin appointed to me as I let out an inaudible sigh of disappointment. I was really hoping that I could stay out of the lime light here. "Where are you going for college, dear?"

"Um, Julliard," I answer softly.

"That's ambitious," Emily, my 25 year old cousin who loves to judge people, pipes as she looks down her nose at me and it is so infuriating that I just look away. "I hardly think that you'd be able to get in though. I mean, Julliard is one of the most prestigious schools in the country, you know."

"Yeah, I know," I confirm with a nod and I bite my tongue to watch my tone so that I don't come off as rude even though she's already pissing me off. "I've actually already gotten accepted and I have a full ride scholarship."

"So do you sing then?" Aunt Theresa asks me, seeming genuinely curious.

I feel a pang of hurt that my mother doesn't talk about me being a dancer. I mean, I go to the most prestigious dance school in the country- one of the best in the world- and next year, I'm going to be going to Julliard. And yet, she doesn't think that it's something to brag about to her family. What would ever be enough for her? "Dance, actually," I respond with a dry throat.

"It's fascinating, really," One of the twins takes off with the conversation.

"Because both Stella and Anthony dance," The other one adds. "Remarkably well, so we hear."

"And they're twins," The first one adds. I can't tell which one is Thing 1 or Thing 2 anymore because they got mixed up so I assign a new number to each one. It is now Agent 3 and Agent 4.

"So fascinating," Agent 3 sighs.

"Well, what do you expect to do after school?" Emily continues to make attempts to shoot me down and I don't know why. I think it's because she likes to feel better than everybody else by shooting other people down. It's not going to work though. "There's not much that you can do with a dance degree."

"There's actually a lot I can do with a dance degree from Julliard," I inform her, trying my hardest to keep my tone polite. "I'm going to try to audition for Broadway maybe. I'm not sure yet."

"Broadway?" Aunt Georgie cackles with disbelief. "That's highly unlikely. Do you know how many people dream of going on Broadway, Stella? Highly unlikely."

"Well, a few minutes ago, it was highly unlikely that I'd get into Julliard too," I point out. "And if it doesn't work out then I'll find something else to do."

"Okay, so Sarah, have you found out if you're having a boy or a girl yet?" Aunt Jackie wonders, looking over at my pregnant cousin.

I feel thankful that the conversation is off of me but I also feel like shit because nothing that I do here matters. My life goals, all of my major accomplishments, everything that I have worked so hard for in my entire life, it all just doesn't matter here. It's a joke to them. I am a joke to them. That's why my mother doesn't talk about me or Anthony to them, because she's embarrassed.

And yet, they praise the twins who are majoring in the nonexistent science of twin telepathy and pee together.

I stand up, not really wanting to be in this room anymore. Just as one of the waiter people come into the room to finally serve the tea, I walk out. I don't make any excuses for it like going to the bathroom or feeling ill, I just leave. I hear my mom call my name and ask where I'm going but I ignore her and keep walking until I'm out of the room and down the hallway a little bit where there seems to be no traffic from the butlers and waiters and maids.

I lean against the wall and let myself fall until my butt is on the carpeted floor and I just think to myself that I'd feel so much better if I could just talk to Andrew.

"Fuck them," He'd tell me. "You're a rock star, Stell."

But he's not here and I want to call him. Even if we're broken up. Even if we haven't spoken in almost a week. I want to call him. I want to hear his voice. I want him to make me feel better because he's the only person in the world that can make me feel better when something like this makes me feel so shitty.

However, even if I had the guts to actually call him (which I don't) I left my phone upstairs in the bedroom that I stayed in last night along with all of my other stuff. I can't decide if that's a bad thing or a good thing.

Either way, I start to cry. I cry because I feel humiliated but that doesn't make any sense. Why should I feel embarrassed? I should be embarrassed that I'm going to one of the best schools in the country? I should be embarrassed that I'm one of the best dancers in the country at my age? I don't know why I feel humiliated, but those women just make all of my achievements sound like crap, as if it means absolutely nothing.

But that's not the only reason that I cry. I start to cry because I realize that the only person that can make me feel better is unreachable. I cannot talk to him. I cannot tell him about my weird and extremely belittling and rude family. I cannot tell him about the strange encounter with the twins.

I want nothing more in this world than to talk to Andrew right now and it hurts so much, so I bend my knees and put my face in my lap as I cry, hoping that the fabric of my dress will muffle my cries enough to not be heard by anybody.

I don't return to the tea room. When I'm done crying, I just hiccup a few times and then find my way back to the bedroom that I had to share with Anthony. I go into the bathroom and look in the mirror, seeing that my makeup smeared a little bit but, because I used waterproof stuff (for this exact reason), it's mostly still in its place.

I don't leave the bedroom after I fix my makeup, I just lay down on my bed and close my eyes. My head hurts from the crying and my heart feels achy and my hands are shaking a little bit too. I doubt that my disappearance from the tea room really disturbed the peace at all, so I don't feel guilty at all by just staying up here for a little while. I don't know how long football games last, but I assume that I have a few hours until lunch. Maybe I'll just skip that too.

Around one o'clock, I decide that I really am going to skip lunch. I know that the butler said yesterday that all events are mandatory today but I don't care. I mean, what are they going to do if I don't show up? Scold me? Lecture me? So what? I'll probably get a lecture for walking out of the tea room unannounced without coming back anyway so it's not like it matters.

However, when there's a knock on the door and I tell it to come in, assuming that it's Anthony coming up to find me once he realized that I didn't go to lunch, I see that my plans to skip lunch are derailed.

"Hey," Jeremy pipes, stepping into the room.

I sit up on the bed and try to find it inside of me to smile at him, but I'm just too tired and my face feels so heavy that I am not strong enough to lift it up into a smile. "Hi. Did they send you to hunt me down?"

"Well, I volunteered," He says. "But they did send me. It's time for lunch."

"Yeah, I don't want to go to that," I inform him. "Send them my deepest apologies."

"I think they really want everyone at the meals," He tells me awkwardly, as if he feels bad for trying to tell me what to do but I know that it's just his job. It's my grandma's fault for having to control everything. What's happening and when it's happening and who is there to engage in whatever it is that's happening. So if there is just one defect, me skipping lunch, that is just not okay at all.

"I feel like I'm in prison," I grumble, combing through my hair with my fingers as I follow Jeremy down the hallway. "I don't get what the big deal is if I don't want to eat lunch with a bunch of whack noodles."

He laughs a little bit. "Well, you're pretty much halfway through the day," He points out. "And then tomorrow, you'll be back on your way- where are you from again?"

"Los Angeles."

"You'll be on your way back to LA in like, twenty-four hours," He explains in a chipper tone. "You can handle it for that long, I think."

"Well, I apparently don't have a choice," I grumble as we walk down the stairs and across the large foyer, probably back into the main dining hall where we had breakfast just so that I can sit down across from the twins and be asked even more invasive questions about climaxes and periods. But it's okay, because it's in the name of science.

"Well, here you go," He says as we walk into the long dining room and everyone is sitting down already, including Anthony, who managed to get two seats in the middle of the table, away from the twins.

"Thanks. You know, for forcing me into my doom. Really appreciate that," I mutter sarcastically as I walk away and sit down between Anthony and Sarah. Across from me is Aunt Georgie and Uncle Denny and then Denny's wife is sitting beside him.

"Hey, what happened?" Anthony asks me. The plates are still empty so I know that I'm not late or anything, which is slightly disappointing because that means that I didn't miss anything.

"Nothing, I just had a moment," I explain to him in a way that really said 'I'll tell you later'.

"Hey, Stella," Sarah says to me from the other side of me. The waiters start to come out to deliver us salad- finally something that I don't mind eating. After they serve all of us our food, they announce that this is the appetizer and the entrée will be out soon. "Congratulations on getting into Julliard. I know that Emily can be a little mean but I think that it's really cool."

I offer her the best smile that I can muster and then mumble a small "Thank you," Before I start eating.

"What's she talking about?" Anthony wonders quietly as I start to eat my salad eagerly.

"I'll tell you later," I assure him.

"It's really cool?" Aunt Georgie overhears Sarah's compliment with raised eyebrows. "It's unproductive."

"What's unproductive?" Anthony asks our rude aunt.

"Julliard," I fill him in.

"It's just such a waste of time and money," She tells me. "I wish you'd choose a better profession, Stella, you have some potential."

"Wait, what?" Anthony wonders in confusion. "You're talking about the big huge famous Julliard, right? The one in New York? Because that's the one that Stella is going to."

"Right," She nods in agreement. "I just think it's a really big mistake for your future."

"Stella's going to be on Broadway," My brother defends me. "And she'll be famous and incredibly rich and it'll be awesome."

I can't help but smile a little bit, but I don't let it show.

"We get free tickets for being family, I hope," Sarah pipes jokingly from beside me and when Aunt Georgie sends her a small glare, Sarah laughs. "What? Broadway is amazing. I'd love to go. Especially if Stella makes it, I think that'd be really cool."

"Denny, would you have tolerated Sarah going off to perform instead of getting a stable degree?" Aunt Georgie drags Uncle Denny into the conversation with Sarah being his daughter and all.

"I will have a stable degree," I interrupt, trying to fend off my annoyance but it's getting harder to do. I start to consider if I'd rather be sitting by the twins. "If I don't make it to Broadway, there's Off Broadway, I could become a dance instructor or a dancer for like, musicians. I could be in music videos- I could tour with Drake."

"Well, if I was your mother, I wouldn't approve," Aunt Georgie informs me. Both Denny and Sarah have adverted to other conversations so it's really just Georgie, me and Anthony talking about this right now and I can tell that Anthony is getting a little bit worked up beside me.

"Well, you aren't my mother and frankly, I don't need your approval," I inform her and this time, it's impossible to hide the irritation from my voice. She's just so condescending and I really can't stand it. Being talked down to is a major peeve of mine and this family has a knack of thinking that they're better than everybody else.

That shuts her up finally and for the rest of lunch, I have a conversation with Anthony and we aren't disturbed again.

10 Thanksgiving- 2

We get a break between lunch and dinner, thank God. After our grandma made the announcement that we have until five to do whatever we want (she hopes that we'll spend it with family) while we wait for dinner, everybody begins to disperse out of the dining hall for the four hour wait. I haven't felt so happy all day.

"We should go up to our room to create a comparison table," One of the twins tells me and Anthony before we can make it out of the room without being noticed. "The differences that you two experienced are quite strange."

"Yes. So strange," The other one agrees. "We must make a comparison table."

"That really sounds like so much fun," Anthony agrees with them jokingly but I know that they don't hear the sarcasm in his voice. "But we have something else to do."

"But it's for science," The first one says as if that means that we have to drop everything and go help them create a comparison table or whatever they want to do. I have a strong feeling that the experiments they want to put me and Anthony through have to do with probes.

"Yeah, and we love science so much," I pipe. "But this thing that we have to do is really important so we'll see you guys at dinner."

Before they can remind us again that we must do this for science, I grab Anthony's elbow and drag him out of the room, towards the stairs so that we can hide out in our room until dinner or maybe find a cool hidden room somewhere that is empty from anybody else.

"Stella," I hear my mom call my name before we get far enough to be considered safe.

I reluctantly turn around to see her coming in our direction, her long brown hair swaying around her shoulders (Anthony and I get our blond hair from our dad although his hair is now gray). "Yes, Mother?" I wonder with an exhausted sigh. Anthony stops with me, thankfully not leaving me alone with our mom. She's not so bad to talk to or anything, I just don't want to be left alone with this family- especially when the twins can creep up at any second.

"I need to talk to you about what happened at tea. And I've been getting some complaints about your behavior at lunch," She explains. "Let's go sit."

"No, I don't need to sit," I shake my head at her. "I know that if somebody 'complained' to you about me during lunch then it was Aunt Georgie. She's just mad because I'm going to Julliard instead of Yale or something. Which makes no sense because nobody in this family has ever made it into an Ivy League school."

"Anthony, do you mind giving us a moment?" She wonders, glancing over at Anthony.

"He can hear whatever you have to say," I assure her and when she gives me a slightly annoyed look, I just shrug. "That's what you get for having twins."

"Fine," She sighs. "We are having a family day, so I'd appreciate it if you honored that and didn't disrespect members of said family, okay? Georgie has very unique standards and I understand that but you still need to respect her."

"I did respect her," I assure my mother. "I snapped at her just a little bit but in my defense, she was talking to me like I was going to school to become a prostitute or something. She was the one disrespecting me."

"She's a total whack job," Anthony adds.

"She's my sister," My mother snaps, sending an offended glare towards him.

"Okay, well your sister is a whack job," Anthony rephrases and I have to stifle a laugh. "It's a miracle that we didn't actually disrespect her. That would make for an awkward dinner."

"Just be nice, that is all I'm asking," She sighs. "It's just one family celebration for one day. Please behave yourselves."

"Is Aunt Georgie like that all of the time? Talking about how terrible it is that Stella is going to Julliard?" Anthony wonders incredulously.

My mom opens her mouth to respond, but I beat her to it. "She didn't know before today. Nobody did. Did they, Mom?" I wonder, referring to how surprised they all were when we were in the tea room and I told them that I dance and that I'm going to Julliard for dance.

My mom closes her eyes and lets out a long sigh as if she's incredibly stressed out right now. "Okay, no, I didn't tell them about Julliard because I know how they'd react. But, Stella, sweetie, that doesn't mean that I'm not proud of you. Your father and I are so incredibly excited for you and we could not be prouder."

"If you were so proud, then you would have told them," Anthony interjects, glaring at our mom.

"Hey," I say softly to stop an argument from coming out of this conversation. "So I have had about literally the worst week of my life and I don't want to make it any worse by fighting right now. I think it'd be best if we just leave early. We can stay at a hotel tonight and then leave tomorrow like planned back to LA. They obviously don't want us here. Except for the creepy twins but they don't really count."

"No, you need to stay," My mother said pleadingly. "You never get to see your family. This is a special time. I'm sorry that I didn't tell them about Julliard, Stella, it's just that they can be very uptight about this stuff."

"I'm not going to go into that dinner just to be berated for following my dreams or looked down upon for doing what I love. That's stupid and I'm not in the mood," I inform her, trying to remain calm but at the end, I can feel myself starting to lose it. My bottom lip quivers but I do not cry. "I just want to go back."

My mom thinks that I just mean that I want to go back to LA but I think that Anthony understands that I mean that I actually want to not only go back to LA, but I want to go back to when I had Andrew and it makes me sound so pathetic, but it's true.

"Look, Stella is going through a lot right now," Anthony begins to explain. "So I think that it's best that we just go now. If you really want to have a family dinner then maybe we can meet up for Christmas or something but right now just isn't the time."

"Stella, what's wrong?" My mom asks me with a concerned frown. "Is everything okay at school?"

"Everything's fine, I just want to go home," I mumble.

She sends me a small smile and then nods in understanding before she steps forward and squeezes my hand in her shoulder. "Okay, I guess I understand. At least say goodbye to your father before you go. I'll tell everyone that you aren't feeling well."

"Sure," I sigh, just glad to get out of this house at an earlier schedule than previously planned. I'm proud to say that I'm a wimp. I just couldn't do it.

"And for the record, I'm really glad to see that you two are finally getting along again after so much fighting," She tells us with a faint smile. "I'll go get your father."

She walks away and I lean against one side of the hallway, hoping that nobody comes down this hallway to try and talk to us. Unless it's Sarah because I love Sarah, but she's probably off with her husband right now so that's unlikely.

"That is one perk of being here," Anthony pipes. "It makes us a little closer- even if it is only for a few days."

"Yeah," I sigh. "It was nice, I guess."

But I know that this Thanksgiving break won't change anything between me and Anthony when we get back to California. We don't fight or anything, but we're distant. We barely ever talk to each other during school because I have my own group of friends and he has his and we just don't get in each other's way at all. After our extremely rough first three years of high school, I think that it's impossible for us to ever be really close for a long amount of time. This terrible family vacation isn't going to change any of that and we both know it. We're going to go back to normal once we get home.

"You're going to leave early?" I hear my dad's voice pipe as he walks down the hallway towards us.

Both me and Anthony nod. "Yeah, I think that's the smartest thing to do right now," I inform him.

"Why is that?" He wonders.

"Because Stella has had a really long week and if they make her cry one more time, I will go off and then Mom will just be even more embarrassed by us and then Stella will go off on them too and it'll just be a big mess. Honestly, it'll be better for everyone if we just leave now," Anthony explains.

"Are Riley and Jamie bothering you guys?" He wonders, referring to the twins by their real names which is something that I rarely do because I can never tell which one is which.

"The Twins, Aunt Georgie, and just…" I'm trying to keep it together but I'm about as emotional as a pregnant lady and I can feel myself wanting to break, but I don't. "It's just everything."

My dad still looks unconvinced that he should let us leave but our mother taps his shoulder and then mumbles, "They're finally getting along, Steven. Let's just give them this one."

"Okay," He sighs, stretching his hand out towards Anthony. "Well, I'm disappointed that you are leaving early."

"Yeah, I guess I've just been disappointing a lot of people lately," I shrug blandly. "Maybe we'll see you guys at Christmas?"

He shakes my hand and offers me a warm smile. "I believe my family will be hosting Christmas. We will see you both there."

My dad's family, in Maine, is so much more normal than my mother's. My paternal grandparents are everything that grandparents should be and it's so amazing and I love them. I see them every Christmas because they have a family Christmas party every year that we fly out to go to and this year will be no different. "Bye then. Love you and happy Thanksgiving," I mutter softly before Anthony repeats almost the exact same thing and after they both mutter an "I love you too" then we turn and go back towards our room.

"That was a lot easier than I thought it'd be," Anthony mumbles as we walk.

"Please," I scoff. "They don't want us here anymore than we want to be here."

"Yeah, that's probably true," He sighs. We go into the bedroom and, since everything is already packed up in our duffel bags pretty much, we just get our stuff and go. "Do you just want to go back to campus?"

"No. Let's just go stay at the airport hotel and relax for the rest of the day and then you can go back to campus tomorrow like planned," I suggest.

"Just me?" Anthony wonders. "What about you?"

"I'm going to stay an extra day. Get a manicure or something, I don't know. I'll just see you back on campus on Saturday. Maybe 24 hours just by myself will do me some good," I explain.

"Sure, if that's what you want," He agrees with me. As we're walking down the hallway, I notice a familiar waiter walking towards the kitchen.

"Jeremey!" I call his name as an idea sprouts in my head out of nowhere. When he hears me, his head turns in our direction and he hurries over to us.

"Hey, what's up?" He wonders before noticing our bags. "Leaving early?"

"Yeah," I sigh heavily. "I ran out of patience halfway through breakfast. Can you do me a big favor?"

"What would that favor be?" He asks me.

"I know that they have an alcohol cabinet or like, an alcohol room or something, right?"

"No," He tells me, already understanding what I'm about to ask him for.

"Please?" I whine softly. "Just one bottle of liquor or vodka or whatever you can get. They won't even notice that it's missing."

"You're still in high school," He reminds me as if I don't already know that.

"Yeah, but this has been one shitty Thanksgiving and it's not like I'll drink the whole thing. Pretty please?" I beg him, hoping to have at least a little bit of fun on this crappy holiday. "I'm not trying to lead you on or anything, because I won't have sex with you for the alcohol, but- Well, okay maybe I'll-"

"No, Stella," Anthony interrupts me with a disapproving shake of his head.

"Okay, yeah you're right," I agree with Anthony and mentally thank him for not letting me do something incredibly stupid in my fits of pathetic sorrow. "But please just one bottle?"

Jeremy sighs, rolls his eyes, and then puts his hand out, "Give me your bag."

I grin and hand him my gym bag, "You're awesome. Thank you so much."

He turns and continues towards the kitchen and Anthony is about to say something before we hear it and it makes us both cringe.

"Stella! Andrew!" One of the twins calls as they both hurry towards us from the opposite direction from where Jeremy just went.

"We heard that you're leaving early," The one on my right tells us.

"But you can't do that."

"Let me guess," I mumble. "In the name of science?"

"Yes," The one to the left nods. "We still have so many questions. The fact that you are two fraternal boy/girl twins is just so fascinating to us."

"We must study you," The other one explains.

"We aren't lab rats," Anthony informs them, his patience wearing thin with these two creep balls.

"Right, but you're our test subjects," The one on the right says. "And you can't leave."

"Since when?" I raise my eyebrows at them. "Don't you have to sign release forms to become test subjects?"

"Well, yes, but this is for science," The left one reminds me for about the tenth time today as if it's the answer to every question that they could ever face. Jump off of a building? Well, if it's for science. Chug a whole jug of spoiled milk? Why not?! It's for science!

"Yeah, but that's the thing," I start to say, losing the rest of my patients for these two wackos just like my brother did moments ago. "We aren't scientists- we are dancers. Artists. Art is the opposite of science in this situation so we, as artists, do not give a flying-"

"What Stella is trying to say," Anthony cuts me off just as Jeremy returns with my gym bag. "Is that she has the flu and we don't want anybody else to get sick so we're just going to leave. Science isn't our top priority right now."

"Thanks," I sigh, taking my gym bag from Jeremy.

"Why did he have your bag?" One of the twins wonders, eyeing Jeremy suspiciously.

"There was a rip in it and he patched it up for me," I explain quickly. "Goodbye, we will see you next year maybe. We're going to go wait for our cab now."

The airport hotel is pretty impressive for an airport hotel, I think. Anthony and I got two separate rooms so that we have our privacy but once we arrived at the hotel, we ordered room service to his room and had a wonderful Thanksgiving dinner together before going down to the pool for a while. It's nice to just spend some time with my brother without our insane family looming over us or anything.

"Don't go crazy with whatever Jeremy gave you, Stell," Anthony warns me as we're walking back up to our rooms wrapped in towels and carrying our clothes.

"I won't go crazy," I assure him. "Are you sure you don't want any?"

He nods. "Yeah, I'm sure. I don't feel like flying tomorrow with a hangover. If you need anything, just come get me or text me or something."

"I'm not going to get shit faced, Tony," I inform him with a small roll of my eyes. "I'm just going to get slightly buzzed. It'll be fine."

"Okay," He sighs. We approach our rooms that are right beside each other and we say goodnight and he tells me that he'll say goodbye to me tomorrow before he leaves for his flight and then we part ways for the night.

I take a shower to get rid of the chlorine in my hair and then get dressed in a large t-shirt and panties before going through my duffle bag to retrieve the bottle of Three Olives Vodka that's supposed to taste like oranges (it says so on the bottle). I'm a wimp when it comes to hard alcohol though, so I take one of the paper cups that the hotel leaves in the room for coffee or whatever and I fill it a fourth of the way full with water and then I pour in some of the clear liquid from the Three Olives bottle.

For a while, I slowly sip at it while watching TV and when it's empty, I'll add more water and more vodka but each time I refill the cup, I put less water into the mixture.

What a life. Getting drunk by myself in the airport hotel. On Thanksgiving. In my underwear. Watching reruns of Home Improvement. I reek of pathetic but that's not going to stop be from stooping even lower.

After my eyes begin to have difficulty focusing on one thing, I figure that I've been sitting around for long enough so I fill the cup all the way with water and sit it on the nightstand so that, as I start to chug the vodka from the long glass bottle, I have a chaser-type thing after I'm done to muffle the burning sensation that's slithering down my throat.

Tonight, I will miss him. I will think of him. I will get drunk and I will cry for him. And then, I will blast my music from my phone and dance around my room as I get too drunk to function. And then I will continue to miss him. It will consume me- every inch, molecule, fiber of my being- until I am brought to my knees, crying hysterically into one of the stark white pillows. Tonight, I will fall apart.

And I do.

I drink and then cry and then I remember Andrew. His scent, his laugh, his soft lips, his calloused hands. The way he says my name like it's a blooming flower. The way he smiles at me and his eyes twinkle. The way he makes me feel- all bubbly and giddy and happy all of the time. I miss that feeling. The fact that I will never feel like that again breaks my heart.

I'm lying on the carpeted floor on my back with a pillow over my face to muffle my cries because everything hurts. Not just mentally, but physically. My whole body just aches.

And then, when I feel like I cannot feel any worse at all, I remember that it is all my fault. I'm the one who broke up with him. I did this. He didn't want to break up, but I did. I was the one who did this to myself, so I shouldn't be crying. This is what I wanted, isn't it? I wanted to break up with him.

But I know that it isn't true. I never wanted to break up with him but I just couldn't take it anymore. It felt like, while we were still dating, he slowly just fell out of love with me. He stopped caring, stopped smiling at me like he used to. He stopped looking at me altogether like I was a ghost in his world that didn't matter anymore. I had no place in Andrew's world anymore and I couldn't take that feeling. It hurts so bad to know that I love him more than anything in this world and yet, he just didn't give a shit about me- he used to, but somewhere in the middle, he stopped.

Maybe it was me or something that I did, but I can't think of anything that I did wrong. I was always there for him but I was never smothering. I was always honest but I was never brutal. I don't know what I did wrong.

Maybe I can just call him and ask him. It's only midnight here which means that it's like ten o'clock over there in New Mexico so he should be able to answer his phone. I can feel it in the back of my skull, my sober self, telling me that it's such a terrible idea to call Andrew right now, but I've had so much to drink that I just don't care.

With a tear-stained face and trembling hands, I grab my phone, stop the music, and dial his number. It rings a few times and with each ring, I get closer to convincing myself to hang up the phone before he really does answer, but I never do.

"Hey, this is Andrew but you've clearly missed me so just leave a message if you want to," The answering machine thing says and I can hear my laughter in the background because I was there when he was recording that after he got his new phone at the beginning of the school year and he was also sitting on top of me, tickling my abdomen with one hand and holding the phone to his ear with the other one.

I start to cry harder as the phone beeps and before I can get myself to hang up, I'm leaving a message. And then I find myself calling him again and again, leaving five consecutive voicemails for the boy who stopped caring but he forgot to give me the memo because I never stopped, I just got left out to dry. Like always. Five voicemails in though, I decide that's enough.

"I'm so drunk right now," I began the first one. "And I'm thinking about you and I know that I shouldn't be but I can't help it. I'm so sorry. For everything."

"I know that you don't want to talk to me right now," Is the second one. "And I know that I shouldn't be calling but I just thought it'd be nice to hear your voice or something. I don't know, I just don't want to be alone anymore."

"I'm so sorry that I wasn't good enough for you," I cried on number three. "I tried the best that I could but I know that it wasn't enough and I'm so sorry. I wish that I could be enough for you- I want nothing more in the world than to make you happy and I'm just so sorry that I couldn't do that."

And after crying for a little while longer, I sober up enough for number four: "I can't sleep because I'm thinking about you and these memories are keeping me awake. I hope that you're thinking about me too."

And the most pathetic (yes, it gets worse), is the grand old number five.

"I miss you."

Picture on the side is Alexander Ludwig, who plays Anthony

11 Panicking

Andrew's POV

"Where's Stella?" I try to make it sound as nonchalant as I possibly can as I approach Mason and Brian, who are sitting in the food court eating lunch on Saturday. With my tray of food, I sit down beside Brian and diagonally across from Mason.

Mason looks at me with a sympathetic frown so I guess my nonchalance wasn't good enough to hide the panic in my voice. I thought that she was supposed to come back to campus yesterday with her brother but when I returned from New Mexico this morning, I noticed Mason and Sienna hanging out without Stella and I passed Anthony on my way to the food court. They were traveling together but only one of them is back.

My first thought is that Stella isn't coming back, which is why I'm panicking. I don't want her to leave school just because of our break up. I don't want her to leave at all. After listening to all of her drunken voicemails yesterday, I realized that maybe it's not over for us. She misses me and, God, I miss her. Maybe I can fix this. If I just apologize, just tell her how I feel, then I can fix this.

I wrote down a few romantic speeches this morning on the flight back to California from New Mexico and after lunch, I was going to go buy some flowers to give her as I do something really romantic to win her back. This past week without her has been driving me crazy. Even back home, the only thing I had to take my mind off of Stella was my older brother, Lucas, who is twenty and he figured that the best way to distract me was to beat me up and tell me to "suck it up and get laid".

I can't keep living like this- endlessly thinking about Stella, hating myself for screwing up everything. I can't even eat all that much without feeling like I'm going to throw it up. I have to get her back. I know that I messed up a lot and took her for granted way more than once but I have to tell her how sorry I am. I have to get her back.

"I don't know," Mason says, bringing me back to the present. "She was supposed to come back yesterday with Anthony but I haven't heard from her at all."

I start to panic even more. What if I pushed her away that badly? What if she's gone for good? I'll... I'll have to find her. She's probably still in Tennessee so I'll just fly there and convince her of how sorry I am about the video games and talking to Charlotte and about everything. I'm so sorry about everything that I ever did to hurt her. I'll tell her that I miss her and that I need her. I'll tell her everything- anything. I just want her back. Back at Vaughn. Back with me. Just back.

"She'll probably be back before Monday when classes start again," Brian assures me with a mouthful of spaghetti. "I mean, really? Do you seriously think that she'd just leave when she's five months away from graduating and going to Julliard? You have to know that she wouldn't do that. She'll be back before Monday."

I let out a long sigh, relieved that Brian just put a lot of sense into my head. He's completely right- Stella wouldn't give up on Vaughn just because we broke up. Her dreams are coming true because of this school and all she has to do is graduate before it all happens. She'll be back.

"Yeah. You're right," I agree with him as I stand up from the table, deciding that I just need to get some air. I can walk down the road to where there's a strip mall with a flower shop in it and I can buy Stella some kind of weird flower because that's something that we've always done. I got her roses once but she said that they were nice, but also so cliché and Stella Wayne is not a cliché girl. So the next time that I got her flowers, I got her some weird yellow thing that looked like a goblin hand. Now, every time I get her flowers, I try to outdo the strangeness of the flower.

On my way down the street, I pass the small ice cream store that sits at the corner of campus and it's kind of busy since it's a weekend and it's the only place that sells ice cream anywhere around here. My chest starts to ache when I remember when Stella and I went there. Well, we used to go there all of the time but there is one particular time that is particularly special.

"Why are you looking at me like that?" Stella wondered, looking at me with bemusement sparkling in her eyes as she licks her ice cream cone. "Do I have something on my face?"

"No," I said but then I realized that there really was some chocolate on her left cheek. "Well, yes, but that's not it. I have to tell you something."

"Okay then," She took her napkin and wiped away the ice cream and continued licking from the cone. "What do you have to tell me?"

I pursed my lips, unsure if that was the place to do it. Maybe she wanted some huge declaration where I took her out to a super nice restaurant and went slow dancing. Maybe that was a mistake but I didn't think that I could not tell her for another minute. She could yell at me later for my terrible timing and nonexistent sense of romance, I was going to tell her. "Stella, I love you."

"Yeah, I love you too," She told me in a breeze, just like she said it all the time, like it was no big deal because we'd been friends forever and we said 'I love you' to each other sometimes.

"No, I mean like, I really love you," I said, acutely aware that my fudge sundae was sitting in front of me melting and going untouched. "Not a friendly kind of love, I really love you. So much."

Her upbeat smile suddenly slackened. She wasn't frowning, but she wasn't smiling either and then she licked her lips to get rid of all of the extra chocolate and then she started to nibble on her bottom lip, which was something that she did when she was thinking about something really hard. She opened her mouth to speak but then shut it again, deciding against saying whatever it was that she was about to say. I clenched a fist under the small table to try and hide my nerves. I just wanted her to say something. Anything. Finally, she looked up at me, her blue eyes seemingly afraid of something and then she opened her mouth and spoke. "I don't want to get hurt," She mumbled under her breath- so quietly that I barely even heard her.

I took her hand in my unclenched one and held it on the table between our melting ice creams and I squeezed tight, trying to assure her that I would never hurt her. I couldn't. Stella was (and still is) the definition of perfect, but she wasn't too perfect. She was so imperfect that all of her flaws were perfect to me. "I would never," I said to her, hoping that she could see the sincerity in my eyes. I knew that there was nothing I could say that could convince her that I wouldn't hurt her because of all that she'd been through previously, so I tried my best to prove it to her by the look in my eye and the squeeze of my hand.

She squeezed my hand back and a smile started to tug at the corner of her quivering mouth and I unclenched my fist under the table, feeling a lot more relaxed. "Well then, Andrew Haggerty, I love you too."

Without even realizing it, I find myself walking towards the ice cream parlor instead of around to the strip mall. I guess it won't hurt to get a milkshake before I head to the flower shop, so I walk inside and I'm immediately hit by the chill of the freezers and the air conditioning inside of the small parlor. I make my way to the counter and order myself a chocolate milkshake, making sure that I don't turn towards the booth that's on the left side of the place. The one that I was sitting in with Stella when I first told her that I loved her. I don't really want to look at it right now. When I realize how ridiculous I sound, I run my fingers through my hair in frustration and then pay for the milkshake and wait for them to make it.

"Shut up, you're lying," I hear somebody say with a loud laugh that drives a shiver right up my spine. Even in the dull buzz of the busy ice cream shop, I can hear the laugh clearly. I know that it's Stella, she's sitting in one of the booths behind me, laughing at something that somebody else just said. I don't want to see her because I'm not ready for my huge romantic gesture yet, but I find myself spinning around in my spot anyway.

I immediately see her curly blonde hair in the crowd, facing away from me, and she's just sobering up from her laugh. I know that it's a fake laugh by how loud it was and I suspect that she's just trying to tell herself that she's happy but I know that she's not. She has to be as miserable as I am. I know that it's terrible to say that, but what we had was real to me and so a week after we broke up, I don't want her to be happy and over it yet. If it meant something to her too, then she'd be miserable still. It makes me sound like a jerk, but that's just how I feel. And by the sound of all of those voicemails I got, I'd say that she's not nearly as happy as she's letting on right now.

Even though Brian reminded me that she was coming back before Monday, I'm still so relieved to see her sitting there because it means that she really wasn't ditching town because of our breakup. In the euphoria of that revelation, I find myself moving forward towards where she's sitting in the booth. However, when I get closer, I stop halfway there, standing in the middle of the shop, staring at the other side of the booth, shocked to see Drew sitting there with her.

Drew was a guy that Stella hung out with before we got together, over the summer. And by hang out, I mean that they would hook up at his house almost every week, sometimes more. They never dated though but I still really don't like the guy and I definitely don't like that he's sitting at the booth with her right now. Maybe it's jealousy- it's definitely jealousy- but I really just want to punch the guy in the face.

I realize that that'd be a really stupid thing to do though, so instead, I turn to walk back to the counter but before I do, I notice Drew look up and notice me. We make eye contact for a moment before he says something to Stella and nudges his head in my direction, causing Stella to spin around and then I'm making eye contact with her and it sucks.

I bite my tongue and tense my jaw just to make sure that she can't see any emotion on my face. Nothing. Although I want to know if she's going back to Drew now that we're done, I'm not going to ask her that. I'll find out, but not directly from her. I'll ask Brian, who will find out from Mason or something.

She looks really embarrassed about something as her face flames red and she looks completely ashamed but she doesn't break eye contact with me and it suddenly feels like the rest of the world has fallen away and we are the only two people on the planet. There is no Drew. There is no arguing or jealousy. It's just us. All of her drunk voicemails start to play in my head again on a loop and I bet that's what she's thinking about right now, which is why she looks so ashamed. Or maybe it's because she's sitting there with Drew, who she hasn't talked to since she broke things off during the summer (or so I thought, I guess). She opens her mouth to speak, but before she gets anything out, I turn back around and grab my milkshake from the counter before taking off out of the ice cream shop.

I don't want to talk to her, especially not right now when she's talking to Drew. I don't know if I'm mad at Stella or myself or both of us or if I'm just mad at everything, but I suddenly feel so mad. How could she be hooking up with Drew just a week after we broke up? How could she do that? I know that they were just sharing ice cream but Drew isn't the kind of guy to just hang out with a girl without it being something more. He's a pervert- he used Stella back then when she wasn't incredibly emotionally stable and now he's using her again. And she's letting him.

I know that it's my fault that we broke up, even though Stella was the one who actually broke up with me. It was all my fault. I really didn't think that the video games bothered her that much, I just thought that when she was complaining, it was just her being a drama queen like she always is. I shouldn't have taken advantage of her like I did though, it just took me way too long to realize how incredibly lucky I was to be with somebody as amazing as Stella. I didn't realize it, actually, until it was too late and she was already realizing that she deserves somebody way better than me.

Outside, I toss the milkshake in the trash can and head back to campus. Without the flowers.

12 More Trouble

"Do you think that he's mad?" Drew wonders from across the booth as we both watch Andrew storm out of the ice cream shop.

"I... I don't know," I mumble in confusion. He looked angry but I'm not so sure why he would be. I'm putting my money on the fact that I'm sitting with Drew right now and he knows about my promiscuous past with the guy. We messed around a lot during the summer, just before I got together with Andrew. If he just stopped and let me explain, I would have told him that I'm only sitting with Drew right now because he walked into the ice cream place as I was eating and decided to sit with me to catch up since we haven't spoken in months. His new girlfriend goes to Vaughn, so he was hanging out with her but on his way back to his house, he decided to stop for ice cream and that's the only reason I'm sitting with him. I wish I could explain that to Andrew.

"If you guys broke up, why would he care though?" He asks as I continue to watch out the window where Andrew is walking back towards campus with his back towards me. I wish that if I just stared at him long enough, I would be able to figure him out, but that's not possible, unfortunately.

"It's complicated," I mumble, standing up from the booth. "Anyway, I should get back to campus and take a nap. I'm finally feeling all of the jet lag from this morning. It was nice catching up, Drew."

"Yeah, you too," He says as I start to leave. We part ways without exchanging phone numbers or planning to meet again because we aren't friends or anything, we just had a thing for a little while about forever ago so it was just a polite little conversation but now, all I can think about is Andrew.

When I get back to campus, I just go up to my room and lay down, really pretty tired from the flight I had this morning. I don't want to think about the extremely long Thanksgiving break I had and I certainly don't want to think about Andrew, so I just lay down on my bed and go to sleep.

I wake up again just after lunch time, which means that I'm very hungry, so I text Sienna and Mason that I'm back and that I'm going to the food court if they want to meet up there for food. They both text me back saying that they already ate but when I'm done, they're all in the game room so I should meet them there.

I agree that I'll be there in half an hour and then slip on some shoes and go to the food court. Because it's not during lunch, the area is pretty empty which means that the lines are pretty short and that's amazing because I hate how terrible the lines get during school.

I breeze through the large salad bar and then sit down at one of the many small two people tables and eat my salad. As I'm walking towards the trash can to throw away my trash, I pass a group of four girls eating tacos and I'm not eavesdropping but it's not like I can just not hear them as I pass.

"You know Andrew Haggerty?" I hear one of them wonder curiously towards another one of them, causing me to inconspicuously start moving slower towards the trash can. There aren't many people in the cafeteria still, so it's easy to hear them even though I'm not incredibly close and it's not like they're trying to talk quietly.

"Yeah, he and Stella just broke up," Another one says. "Why?"

"He's outside with that new chick right now," The first girl says. "The British one with the twin."

"Nel, you're just looking for trouble," One of the other girls says. "It's probably nothing."

I speed up now, walking past the table to throw away my trash. They all look over at me, finally realizing that I'm in hearing range and all four of them pale a little bit, looking petrified that their conversation wasn't as private as they thought it was. Ignoring their mumbles and gasps, I hurry towards the exit of the food court to look for Mason.

If he is talking to Charlotte then I don't want to see it. I don't want to believe that Charlotte won whatever twisted game she's been playing. I just want to hide out in the dorm with Mason and Sienna and watch movies and stuff. I don't want to think about Andrew or Charlotte or how I'd be able to stand it if they got together.

However, I'm forced to think about it when, as I'm passing the center fountain in the middle of the school, I see them. That gossiping girl was right- Andrew and Charlotte are sitting on one of the benches near a large tree. They're sitting very close together too, and she's laughing at something he just said with her hand resting lazily on his forearm.

I don't even realize it until I feel the pinch of my nails digging into my palms, but my hands are clenched into fists by my sides and I've stopped walking. They're pretty far away, so they don't notice me standing there at first, which is good, because I need some time to just stare.

I'm not really mad that he's talking to Charlotte- I realize that I don't have any right to be mad about who he talks to anymore. The issue isn't really Charlotte at all, actually. It just hurts- it really fucking hurts- that he's sitting there, letting her flirt with him, as if we didn't break up just a week ago. As if we meant nothing.

They probably aren't actually dating (I don't know if I'd ever be able to deal with that) but he sure doesn't seem completely against that idea by the way that they're sitting- the way that she's leaning into him like putty on his shoulder. It's disgusting.

I want to move, to leave the large center yard of campus and go to Mason and Sienna and rant to them about how much I hate Charlotte, but I can't. I feel paralyzed as my lungs deflate and then refuse to inflate again. They become numb just like the rest of me but I can feel my throat constricting and then I'm having trouble breathing.

In and then out, breathe in and then out.

I don't know how long that I'm standing there until Andrew notices me. He looks up from laughing at something that Charlotte had said, and then when he sees me standing there, Charlotte notices him staring so then she looks up too. Andrew and I maintain eye contact for a long time and it makes my belly do a little flip. She says something to him but he still doesn't take his eyes off of me, and then he shrugs. Keeping his eyes on mine, he slides his hand up so that instead of holding onto his forearm, Charlotte is holding his hand. Interlocking their fingers together, he begins to glare at me.

A glare that shatters me again. The bits of me have been shattered again and now, I'm even smaller. It's like I'm a mirror that had fallen over and broke into a few hundred pieces but now, a giant has come along and stomped all over me, breaking even the broken parts into even littler, even more broken parts. I have no idea why he's glaring at me like that, why he's suddenly angry at me for something. I have no idea why he would want to hurt me like that.

I'm sure that the amount of pain that I'm suddenly feeling shows on my face because a second after the glare, his face softens into a sympathetic frown and then, before I can see anything else, I turn and walk towards the dorms. There's nothing I want more right now than to be able to get out of there as fast as I can, to just sprint to the dorms, but I will not let them know how much they got to me. I walk, counting my steps at a deliberate pace so that I know that I'm not walking to quickly to qualify as normal. Because I am normal.

At least, that's what I tell myself until I'm in the safety of the dorm and then I hurry into the game room. Mason and Sienna are both in there so I lock the door behind me and then sit down on the couch between both of them.

"Stell…" Mason says slowly, obviously noticing that something is wrong by the way that I entered the room. "What happened?"

I open my mouth to tell her something 'he's over me' or 'he's with Charlotte' or something along those lines but when I open my mouth to speak, the only thing that comes out is an unexpected sob. How could he do that? How could he just act like we meant nothing? Like everything that we'd been through in these past months has all been a complete lie? How can he want to hurt me like that? I just don't understand what's happening right now.

Sienna puts her hand on my shoulder, preparing to ease me out of a very long, very painful session of sobs and crocodile tears, but they never come. There's just one dry sob and then I'm done. I'm not going to cry over him like a pathetic little love sick puppy. That's what I want to do, but I won't let myself stoop that low right now. I'm going to convert all of the sadness and pain I feel right now into anger.

"I'm going to go," I mutter shakily, standing up from the couch without even explaining anything.

"What? Stella, what's going on?" Sienna wonders curiously in a concerned voice.

"Just Andrew," I sigh, offering them a small wave before leaving the game room.

"Stella, wait, talk to us," Mason calls as they both follow me out of the room and towards the bank of elevators.

"He's just flirting with Charlotte," I say with a forced shrug. "No big deal, since we're not dating anymore and everything."

"He's what?" Sienna wonders incredulously.

We all walk into the elevator as it opens and then I turn to face them. "They're outside. And the way he looked at me... I don't know what I ever did to make him so mad. He has to be flirting with her just to piss me off, right? That has to be why."

I don't know what they say after that, my ears begin to ring with the rage that's pent up inside of me as I replay the scene from outside in my head again and again and again until I feel like my forehead is going to cave in due to the pressure inside of my head.

When I leave Sienna and Mason concerned in the dorms, I head to my car. There's a gym on campus but it's very neglected considering we spend most of our time working out here so it doesn't really make sense for us to want to spend our free time working out as well. The gym in downtown Oxnard is really nice though, so I go there and purchase a day pass because I barely ever go here and I'm not going to buy an actual membership for something that I rarely ever do.

So I go inside and find the boxing stuff. There's those little bags that look like tonsils, those cylinders that stand on a sand bag or something and then when you punch it, they spring back into your face, and then there are the super heavy punching bags, which are what I'm looking for.

I don't know much about boxing, but it's something that helps me vent some of my unwanted emotions sometimes. I'd rather be punching Charlotte or, at the moment, Andrew, but this is a better way of doing that, and it also prevents me from getting suspended or something, which could possibly put my Julliard scholarship in jeopardy or something.

There are instructor people walking around the wide open space, so I ask one of them to help me wrap my hands in the white gauze tape or whatever it's called, and then I go over to one of the softer punching bags and start going at it.

The only thing that I can think of as I'm throwing punch after punch after punch is that look that Andrew gave me as he pulled Charlotte's hand into his own. Daring me to show any type of emotion. The way he looked at me- that ruthless glare, I just don't get it. I know that he was doing it to hurt me- or to piss me off- but he was trying to start something. I don't know why, or why he was even talking to Charlotte or why any of that just happened. Even if he was only sitting with her to piss me off, it still makes my stomach churn.

I punch the bag in front of me with thud after thud and as I continue, I feel my rage begin to build up instead of calming down like it usually does. I keep seeing Andrew's face, glaring at me, as he's holding Charlotte's hand and letting her mindlessly flirt with him. I keep feeling that fire continue to burn in the bottom of my belly and it keeps growing until there's a wildfire burning on my skin, searing me as if my sweat is gasoline.

Maybe it was just a ploy to piss me off, but it still hurts like hell to see him with her. I don't want to see him with somebody else like that, like we didn't even matter at all. I don't want to even believe that there is a possibility that he's already moving on from us. I want him to hurt and I know that it seems terrible but I do. I want him to hurt, to show me that we actually meant as much to him as we did to me.

I keep punching the bag, feeling the burn on my skin fuel the rage I feel towards Andrew and Charlotte and that stupid glare and all of this stupid crap.

"Hey, stop," I hear one of the instructor's say, approaching my side, but I ignore him, deafened by the now consuming rage I feel towards everything- including myself. "Ma'am, no. Stop."

When I don't stop punching the bag on my own, he reaches over and grabs one of my wrists in his big muscly hands, which is when I finally stop throwing punches at the bag.

"You need to take a break. Okay?" He says, holding my hand up so that I can see the blood seeping through the tape on my knuckles. "Do you want some ice?"

"No," I breathe, panting from all of the physical exertion I just put on myself. "Sorry. I'm, uh, I'm fine. Thanks."

The man gives me a strange look but I just turn, grab my bag, and hurry out of the gym again. Once I get to my car again, I regret not taking the ice that was offered to me because I can feel the burn on my knuckles now. I unwrap my hands and cringe at how bloody both of my hands are from how hard I was punching the bag. This is going to be a long drive back to campus.

And it is. After I get back to campus, I go to the nurse's office to get my hands iced and then wrapped. Apparently, I almost sprained my left wrist, so the nurse put an actual wrap on my wrist and then sanitized and wrapped my bloody knuckles in bandages before she gave me the 'okay' to go leave the nurse's office.

It's about dinner time now, but I'm really not hungry, I'm just exhausted and grumpy and I want to go back to my dorm and maybe cry a little bit and try to figure out my life and what the heck I'm going to do next.

I numbly walk towards my room, fighting to take each step with just how tired of this I am. I'm tired of feeling tired and drained and angry and sad and empty. I'm tired of it all. Up the elevator and then down the hallway, I'm almost to my room when I stop dead in my tracks. Andrew is sitting there, right beside my door with his back leaning against the wall and his head resting in his palm with his elbow resting on one of his bent knees.

My keys jingle in my hand as I stop, which he hears, and then he looks up at me. We make eye contact again and I flinch, recalling that the last time we made eye contact, he was glaring at me with a look that I could only recognize as hatred.

I don't care anymore though- at least, I really try not to- and I ignore him as I start to go for my door again, scrambling with my shaking hand to get my room key in my fingers. Andrew scrambles up to his feet and intercepts my straight path to my door, but he doesn't say anything. He's probably looking at me, I can basically feel his eyes drilling holes into the top of my head, but I don't look up at him. I just look at his broad shoulder, forcing myself not to look up at his face because I don't want to see him. I don't want him here right now. I don't want to talk to him, I just want to pretend that he doesn't even exist. That he never existed. I don't even move or try to push past him. I will not give into his attempt to make me recognize that he's here, I just stand there, calmly waiting for him to move or say something or just do something.

"I'm so glad that you're okay," He finally breaks the silence with a voice that's just a little over a whisper. "I looked for you all over campus. I was so worried, Stell."

I don't move at all until he says my name and it still sounds like an angel coming down from heaven, just to say my name. It's magical, and the nostalgic feeling that smacks me in the face makes me cringe. I still don't speak, I just remind myself to keep looking at his shoulder and just stay calm. He'll move eventually and I don't want to talk to him.

"I know that I took things too far. I'm sorry, okay?"

I still remain silent and I mentally applaud my solid resolve.

"Stella, please just say something. Talk to me. Please," He begins to plead in a soft voice and then he puts his hand on my shoulder and I take a step back, not wanting him to touch me at all. I miss his touch like crazy and it makes me so mad. It makes me so mad that I'm not completely disgusted by him. It makes me so mad.

"I don't know what you're talking about," I finally mumble in a shaky breath, finally unable to stand his scrutinizing gaze.

"I know that you do," He counters and I can hear the relief in his voice that I just spoke, which makes me regret ever talking at all. Not just right then, but forever ago, when I was just meeting him, I regret that I ever said 'hello' to him at all. My life would be so much easier right now if Andrew Haggerty was not a part of it.

"I hate you," I whisper with my eyes closed because I know that if they were open, Andrew would realize how untrue that is. He'll never know how true that I want it to be though, or how badly I want to hate him.

"No you don't," He argues, already able to catch my lie, which is completely unfair. I hate that he can read me like that. I hate that he thinks that saying sorry will fix everything. I hate everything about him, actually, but I just can't find it in myself to actually hate him.

"But I want to," I say, still whispering with a quiver because I know that if I try to talk right now, I'll just lose it. All of my composure will just be gone. "So much. And it's really unfair."

"But you don't," He repeats.

"Shut up," I say, really not wanting to hear his stupid voice anymore.

"Stella, please,-"

"It was Drew, wasn't it?" I wonder curiously, keeping my eyes stuck on his shoulder as I ask the question when I remember that he saw me sitting with Drew at the ice cream shop earlier. That's probably what this is all about. He thought that I was moving on or something so he wanted to show me that he was also moving on. With Charlotte, just to make it sting that much more.

"Stella,-"

"I hate you," I say again. "And I don't want you to talk to me again, okay? Ever. Just stop. Seriously. None of it even matters anymore," I mutter as I push him violently away from the door and then I stab my key into the door and then unlock it, turning quickly into the room before Andrew can say anything else.

"Stella, I'm sorry!" He calls through the door, knocking three times before realizing that I'm not going to answer him.

I'm too busy stuffing my face into a pillow and crying my stupid little eyes out.

13 Avoiding Him

"So can you still dance with your wrist wrapped up and everything?" Brian wonders as we're sitting down for breakfast on Sunday morning. I'm not sure why we're having breakfast together, just me and him, but we're close friends so it's not like I'm complaining. It's just weird though, since I usually eat breakfast with Mason and Sienna.

"Yeah, it feels spectacular," I assure him. "I worked out on it yesterday with like pushups and stuff like that and it felt fine. The nurse said that it wasn't anything big, she just wrapped it to help with the pain."

"What'd you do again?" He asks. "To hurt your wrist, I mean."

I shrug. "Lost my temper for a little while, with good cause, and it just got bad. I'm fine though, it's no biggie. Where's your girlfriend? Or Sienna?"

"They're talking to Andrew," He supplies. "Don't ask me why or what they're talking to him about because I don't know, that's just what Mason told me."

I roll my eyes at him. "They're probably trying to yell at him because he's such a stupid person."

"Did something else happen?" He asks me cluelessly. "In the past few days, I mean. I didn't really talk to him at all yesterday."

"Yeah, I don't want to even think about it though, so let's just talk about something that's not Andrew related, okay?"

"Sure," He agrees. "How was your Thanksgiving break?"

"Just as insane as I thought it would be. My family is full of weirdoes and pretentious snobs who don't approve of me going to Julliard, so that was fun. And then the twins, who were probably plotting a way to steal a piece of my hair or cut off my tongue or something in the name of science."

"Wait, what?" He laughs. "Your tongue?"

I nod and then try to explain everything about the twins, laughing as I go. Sure, they're super annoying when I actually have to deal with them but when I reflect back on the situation, I can definitely find hilarity in their personalities. I tell him all of the weird and creepy things that the twins had asked me and Anthony- like how they asked if I felt an attraction for Gianna and how they wondered if Andrew could sense my menstruation.

"Wait," Brian says with a long laugh. "So they actually made you go to the bathroom together?"

"Yes!" I laugh. "It was so weird. And they tried to get us to like, do experiments or something, but we got the hell out of dodge before that happened."

"I want to meet these people," He tells me, finally sobering up from laughing at all of the weird things the twins had done over break.

"No, you really don't. It's exhausting and extremely creepy," I warn him. "They're a nightmare to be around. They wanted us to fly back to Tennessee for extra experiments next weekend but I'd rather cut my own face off than have those two creeps do experiments on me and my DNA."

"Well, your break was a lot more eventful than mine, it seems, because all I did was go to dinner with my family and then I just hung out with Mason the rest of the time, which was nice," Brian tells me with a shrug.

After that, we decide that it's about time to go to class, so we stand up from our table in the food court and throw away our trash in the closest bin thing and then we leave the food court, going towards the academic building. I don't really know where his first period class is, but we'll walk as far as we can together and then just split ways.

"I wish that thanksgiving break was longer though," I say as we're walking towards the building with a lot of other people who are starting classes right now. "I'm not ready to go back to school and everything."

"I don't think anybody is ever ready to go back to school, Stell," He chuckles.

"Yeah, that's true. English is really going to suck ass though," I sigh, wondering if it's even possible for me to make it through that class, the one that I have with Andrew not including dance, alive. "And in dance, I'm going to be glued to your side, so stay away from him. He'll probably be with Charlotte anyway."

"Charlotte?" Brian repeats in confusion.

I shrug. "It's a story. I'll see you at lunch," I say before turning down another hallway to get to my class just so that I can avoid talking about what happened on Saturday with Andrew and Charlotte. I haven't talked to anybody about it at all, actually, because I just really hate even thinking about it. That's probably why Sienna and Mason are talking to Andrew this morning, to see if he'll tell them what happened.

When I sit down in calculus, Sienna is already there, sitting in the chair right beside mine where she always sits.

"He told us what happened," She says without even a 'good morning' or a 'hello'.

"Did he?" I raise an eyebrow at him.

"Yeah, and it was really shitty of him to do that to you," She tells me. "Do you want me to tell you what he said?"

I sigh, knowing that I should say no but I nod anyway. "Yeah, go for it."

"Okay, well he's freaking out a lot because he feels terrible about hurting you so much and he feels really guilty about your wrist and everything."

"He should feel terrible," I mutter.

"I know. He should," Sienna agrees. "He's not actually with Charlotte though. You know that, right? I mean, I'm not advocating for him or anything and I understand that it kind of sounds like that right now, but I just think that you should know that it wasn't real. You probably already know that though, right?"

I nod. "Yeah, I kind of figured."

"I'm really sorry that all of this is happening, Stella," She says sympathetically. "How's your wrist?"

"It's fine," I assure her. "Just a little sore but I can still dance and everything so it's not really a big deal. How's Penn?"

She understands that I just don't want to talk about Andrew anymore, so she offers me a small smile and then starts talking about her own boyfriend. "He's okay. He's been pretty worried about his sister lately though, Ana."

"The one that was in rehab?" I wonder, trying to remember what little bit of Ana that I've heard from Sienna. Penn's family is a very private topic, so I don't really know that much about them at all. I do know that his little sister Ana has been in and out of mental facilities for a few years, though, because she's depressed or something.

"Yeah, well he's worried that she's going to do something to make them put her back in there. I think she'll be fine, but he's worried about her," She explains. "She seems really happy to me."

"All of these years in and out of those hospitals, I'm sure she's really good at faking it," I say. "But what do I know?"

"I guess that's true," She agrees. "It's all just tense right now, I guess."

I listen to Sienna talk about Penn and what they're planning on doing for Christmas and New Years, which seems really romantic- spending Christmas with their families and then taking a trip to the mountains for the New Year.

Class starts soon and then we listen to a lecture on domains and integers and math things like that until it's time for next class, which is psychology. I'm kind of dreading that class considering Charlotte is in there and I just know that she's going to say something and gloat that she won- she won Andrew and which means she won over me. And if she doesn't talk to me, I know she'll be giving me a 'I won' glare the whole class period. I know that this wasn't a game, this whole charade with Andrew, but I also know that that's all this is to her. A stupid game.

I sit with Benji and Sara like I always do and make sure that I never look in Charlotte's direction even though Sara tells me that she is in fact over there and yes, she's looking over in my direction just waiting for me to look up at her, but I won't. I'm not going to amuse her childish whims or whatever they are. Not right now when I have bigger fish to fry than some brat who thinks that she can just take over everything.

"She's really not looking away," Benji tells me as we're working on a worksheet that the teacher had given us. "It's extremely creepy."

"Do you want me to go talk to her?" Sara wonders. "Because I totally will."

"No, it's fine. Just ignore her. I'm sure she'll get bored eventually," I say with a small shrug, still not looking up. I'm not really worried with this period as much as I am worried about going to my English class this afternoon though, so I don't spend any of my energy worrying about Charlotte or how much I want to just punch her in the face or push her over a cliff.

Choreography goes by much faster than psychology did because I don't really talk to anybody in there so then I go to lunch and grab my food but I don't sit with my large table of friends because I see Andrew sitting there on the end between Brian and another one of their friends. Just seeing him right now makes me want to vomit so before I can completely lose my appetite, I turn around and walk outside, deciding to find a place in the grass to sit and eat my food. I almost expect him to walk outside to try and talk to me, or maybe Sienna or Mason to come out and try to cheer me up or go into lunch with them, but none of them come out to speak to me. I'm thankful that Sienna and Mason know just exactly what I need right now- just some time to be alone.

But then, lunch is over and as I stand up, I wipe away the grass that has stuck to the back of my bare thighs (I'm wearing jean cut offs) and then I start my walk into the academic building to go to English. My knees are weak and my hands are shaking because I'm so nervous as I walk. I don't know how I'm going to act to sitting next to Andrew for this whole class period. I don't know if he's going to talk to me or not and if he does, I'm not sure if I'm going to respond to him or not. I have no idea what's going to happen, but I'm tempted now more than ever to skip this class and just wait it out in my dorm until it's time for anatomy.

I don't do that, however, I just get to the English room and sit down in my assigned seat, counting the seconds down until Andrew gets there and I hope that Mason gets there before he does, that way I at least have Mason to help me through this. That dream is short lived, though, because before either one of them arrive, I get this text:

I have a physical therapist appointment in ten minutes. Tried to reschedule but they're completely booked. So sorry- you gonna be alright?

It's from Mason, so she won't be in English at all and I feel my stomach plummet even more. Maybe I actually am going to vomit. I can't do that, though, because I already passed out so if I throw up too, they probably won't let me practice for a while and that's just not okay.

I'll be okay. Have fun

I can skip it if you want

No, don't. really, I'm okay

I know that she knows that it's a lie, but we both know that she can't just not show up to a physical therapy session because they're both expensive and almost impossible to book. She texts me back saying that she loves me and I tell her that I love her too and then I put my phone away because the bell is about to ring. Andrew isn't here yet so hopefully he's just not going to show up, but I know that won't be the case.

Just a few seconds before the bell rings, he proves me right, stepping through the threshold of the doorway and into the room. He walks across the room and sits down beside me where he always sits and I make it a point to keep my eyes glued to my desk. I will not look at him no matter what. I can't do that.

But something that I can't help is the smell. The smell of peppermint and a small hint of Axe fill my nostrils due to his close proximity and a sense of uneasy nostalgia washes over me and I want to vomit again, but I just push it all away and keep my gaze locked on the desk. To prevent my hands from shaking too much, I rest them on the desk and clench them into fists while I wait for class to really start.

I lean forward, resting my elbows on the desk and then I hide my face in my hands. I'm not sure why I do this but I think that maybe if I hide my face from him then he just won't be able to see me at all and then this period will go by so much easier since he won't be able to see me and then all conflict will be resolved. Well, not really but I wish that it was that simple.

"I think that we should talk," Andrew whispers over to me, almost too soft for me to understand what he just said.

I just shake my head, not wanting to verbally speak to him at all. It seems childish but I just can't do it. I'm sure that if I even tried to speak right now, I'd lose any mental control that I have and I'll just start crying like crazy and then I'll embarrass myself in front of this whole class.

"Stella, please," He mutters pleadingly beside me but I just run my fingers through my hair, completely ignoring him this time. I can't do it. I can't do any of this. I'm going to fall apart. "Stella."

"Okay, we're going to get started now," Jackie announces with perfect timing as she starts class. I feel fortunate that she doesn't feel like having a class discussion today like she does a lot of the time, she just starts a documentary about Shakespeare and when we watch videos, she doesn't like people talking or anything which means that this period should be a lot easier than I'd originally thought.

Well, that's what I think until I see Andrew begin to write on a piece of notebook paper in his notebook. The room is dark because Jackie turns off all of the lights but the large projector is shining enough light to allow him to write comfortably.

I try to focus my attention mostly on the video, even though it's incredibly boring, but it's better than looking over at Andrew and wondering what he's writing. When he's finished writing whatever it is that he's writing though, he makes it kind of difficult for me to ignore him by ripping the paper out of his notebook and sliding it over onto my desk.

Without even looking down at the paper, I reach out and crumple up the paper on my desk. I really want to read it- the curiosity is killing me and he knows it- but I remember that glare that was on his face as he held Charlotte's hand just 48 hours ago, and that fuels me to just crumple up the paper and toss it into the trash bucket behind our desks.

It doesn't deter him though, he just rewrites the message on another piece of paper and slides it over to me.

This time, I consider looking down at it- he isn't going to stop anyway, so I might as well just amuse him and read the stupid letter. Very reluctantly, I look down at the paper and read his scribbled handwriting.

I'm sorry about Saturday.

That's it, but I know that just by looking at it, I'm now part of his stupid conversation, so I pick up my mechanical pink pencil and start writing down a short response.

Yeah.

After I slide the paper back over to him without even looking away from the stupid documentary, he looks over at me and then back down at the paper. After writing another short message, he sends it back to my desk.

Can I make it better?

I choke on a silent sob and bite my lip so that I don't actually start crying or anything as I respond.

No.

And then he quickly writes back but I notice that his handwriting is getting even messier. When I look over at him, I can see that it's because his hands are shaking a little bit.

Please.

Looking down, I see that my hands are shaking as well so I move them to my lap so that Andrew can't see them as I consider what I should write back- or if I should write anything at all. Any contact with Andrew feels like both the worst thing in the world and yet, it also feels like the best. I want to be with him forever and yet, I want nothing more than to run away for all of this. From all of him.

I don't know what you want from me.

I slide it back to him and then he quickly responds.

I just want you to listen

And then I write my response and slide it back to him, my hand shaking so badly that I wonder if my handwriting is even legible anymore.

I think I'm done with that

I can see him look over at me from my peripheral vision but I keep my eyes firmly fixated on the overhead at the front of the room. I can't look at him or I really will lose it.

I know that I don't deserve it, but please just listen one more time

I run my fingers over the graphite letters that he just slid in front of me and then, like I did the first time, I crumple up the discussion and toss it into the trash bucket, making it clear that I won't be listening to anything else that he has to say. I can't give in so easily to Andrew- especially after everything that he's done- all of the pain that he's caused me.

For the rest of class, Andrew leaves me alone but I keep shaking, wondering if it were possible for me to forgive him like I so badly want to. I think that the answer to my question, however, is no. No, I will never be able to forgive him for everything that he's done to me before and after we've broken up.

When the bell rings, I'm the first one out the door, just hoping that Andrew doesn't press the subject again after class by following me through the hallways. Luckily, he apparently understands that there will be no progress made if he just forces his way towards me and just leaves me alone as I make my way towards my next class. I'm almost running through the hallways towards Anatomy to get away from Andrew, letting the distance between us calm me down a little bit. Like there's a string between us and as I walk farther away, that string gets thinner and thinner but it will never snap and the thinner the string gets, I feel like I can finally breathe again.

After anatomy, though, that string starts to come back but this time, it's not stretching out, it's retracting. We have dance together and that would be way better than having English together since we don't actually have to stand next to each other when dancing. What sucks most about dance is the fact that both Andrew and Charlotte are in this class. I'm not entirely sure what's going to happen between any three of us. Is Charlotte going to try to talk to me? Or is she going to try and seduce Andrew again? Will it work? It hurts to know that I don't even know the answer to that.

When I get into the classroom, Anthony is with me since we walk together and then Brian walks over to me when he sees me walk in across the room.

"Hey," He smiles at me.

I offer him a wobbly smile in turn. "Hey."

He wraps an arm around my shoulders and starts to walk me away from Anthony, so I just wave at my brother and keep walking with Brian. It feels like that string between me and Andrew is now wrapping around my neck and suffocating me. I hate it so much even though it's a feeling that I used to love.

"Nothing is going to happen with Charlotte," He tells me once we're walking towards the locker rooms since I still have to get dressed in my work out clothes. "He feels really bad about what happened."

"He should feel bad about what happened," I huff before going into the girls' locker room and getting changed into my work out clothes. I shove everything else into my gym bag and then I hurry back into the dance room to find Brian again.

"So are you going to talk to him?" Brian asks me.

I shake my head. "Not anytime soon, no I'm not."

"Okay, well he really wants to talk to you, if that's not been obvious already," He says.

"Yeah, I know," I sigh. "But I'm pissed so I don't really want to talk to him at all."

"I get that," Brian tells me. "And don't think that I'm on his side or anything. I'm trying my best to not pick sides even though he's being really stupid right now. All of this is pretty suckish."

"Very suckish indeed," I agree, leaning my back against one of the cinder block walls. "It'll all blow over eventually though, right?"

"Sure," He appeases me but I can tell that he's not so convinced. To be honest, I'm not either.

Once practice actually starts, I stand beside Brian and then Andrew is on the other side of him, which is better than standing directly beside him like I assumed he would do. Looking around for Charlotte, I see her standing a few people over from Andrew with her eyes staring straight to the front of the room so I have no idea what her deal is. This is going to be an interesting class.

It's actually not so interesting after all. Charlotte keeps her distance from both me and Andrew and Andrew keeps his distance from me, which is exactly what I want. Almost until the end, everything runs as smoothly as possible but then, about forty minutes into class, Charlotte approaches Andrew as Mr. Lynch announces that we have a five minute break. They're pretty far away and other conversations are echoing through the room, so I have no idea what she's saying to him, but he just glares back until she's finished talking and then he says something in return. Whatever they're talking about, it doesn't seem like a pleasant conversation.

I tell myself that it's none of my business and then turn around to ignore them both. I don't care. I don't care at all.

At the end of the five minute break, I stand up from where I'm sitting with Brian and Anthony and as we walk into line, I see Charlotte still conversing with Andrew.

"Don't worry about it, Stell," Brian assures me when he notices me looking at them talk. The only thing that's keeping me sane right now is the fact that Andrew is frowning, obviously unhappy to be talking to Charlotte, which makes me feel a little relieved, I guess.

"I'm not worried," I deny shakily. "It's none of my business who he talks to."

He pats me on the back, rolls his eyes, and then starts walking over to Andrew. They're close enough to Anthony and I that I can hear what Brian is saying to Andrew as he approaches, so I listen.

"Dude, you gotta walk away. You're pissing Stella off," Brian tells him, disregarding Charlotte's existence right beside them.

Andrew looks confused, glancing from Charlotte to Brian and then to me, which makes me look away until he turns back to Brian so I turn and watch the altercation again. "It's not like that though. I'm just telling her that nothing's actually going to happen," He explains, motioning towards Charlotte.

"Yeah, well just walk away, alright? That's not what it looks like to her and you obviously don't want to make her even madder," Brian explains just as it's about time to get back into line for practice again. I make it a point for myself to just completely ignore Andrew for the rest of class even though I know that it won't be easy.

14 Talking

Two weeks go by and nothing gets easier. If anything, it gets much worse by the way that everybody gets so cheery for Christmas. In the middle of December, Santa Clause always visits on the weekend (he's just some football player from the normal high school (OHS) that visits dressed as Santa Clause and then he gets laid) and it's stupid but everybody still gets pretty excited about it. Not only is the idea of Christmas getting people excited, but the fact that we're just one week away from winter break is what's really getting everybody going. Two and a half weeks of no classes, no early mornings, no anything.

The only thing to stress about now is the winter show, which is a recital-type thing that we do on the Friday before break starts and it's open to the public even though mostly just parents and college scouts show up. It's not really a big thing to stress about, so the excitement of the break and the holidays are way more permeating and annoying than the stress.

As for Andrew and Charlotte, I haven't seen them talking at all, which is nice, but Charlotte does glare at me every chance that she gets. It's pretty annoying, but I guess I can deal with it. I don't really care about her as long as she's not talking to Andrew. I know that sounds ridiculous and unfair considering we're broken up but that doesn't mean that I want to see him with anybody else. At least not anytime soon. I haven't talked to Andrew either, but we do glance at each other every once in a while and Brian keeps me updated on him even though there's really not that much to be updated about. He got accepted to a few colleges, he's going home for Christmas, he still talks about me. That's about it.

And I wonder if Brian tells him about me. I wonder what he tells him, even though there's really nothing going on in my life. I signed up for my dorm in Julliard. I talked to my mom. I still wake up in the middle of the night, crying for Andrew like a little kid waking up from a nightmare and crying for their mother. Then again, nobody really knows about that one except for the people on either side of my dorm who probably hear me crying and/or screaming.

"So the Santa this year is a junior from OHS," Mason informs me on Friday- just one more week until winter break.

"People here really get into Santa coming?" Sienna wonders with a small laugh.

I nod but I haven't been in much of a talkative mood lately, so I let Mason explain. "It's pretty funny because it's a different person every year and we hardly ever have any contact with OHS- it's kind of a rivalry of sorts- and this guy is almost always either a little high or a little drunk but not too much to where he attracts the attention of the teachers or anything. So then he goes around hitting on girls- 'do you wanna sit on my lap'- type of things and it's all in good fun, it's not harassing or anything. And then eventually, one of the girls will go with him and then ho ho ho."

"Wow. That's kind of weird," She says. We're sitting down in the food court for dinner while the guys are hanging out with each other. After we have dinner though, Sienna is going to go spend the weekend with Penn and then I'll probably be stuck having a movie marathon by myself if Mason goes off with Brian like she does on weekends. It's not like I'm mad about that or anything- just because I'm not in a relationship doesn't mean that my friends shouldn't be happy in their relationships- but it just sucks being alone all of the time. I didn't really realize how much time I spent with Andrew until I had to start spending my time avoiding him.

"It's really weird," I add to the conversation. "But it's just one of those stupid traditions that everyone insists that we keep doing."

"I think it's cute," Mason shrugs.

"Well, I think it'll be interesting to see," Sienna chuckles with a mouthful of macaroni and cheese.

"Speaking of interesting, I have practice until four tomorrow for that holiday show next weekend," Mason pipes, changing the subject a little bit. The winter show has a bunch of different acts because it's not like they could fit our whole school onto the stage at once but it's a required show, so everyone has to participate on stage. They have different acts and different types of music that people can dance to so the show tells an actual story. Mason and Sienna are doing lyrical but they're two different lyrical parts, so they don't practice together, and then I'm doing jazz just because I'm not too good at jazz and I like to challenge myself. Each instructor at the school is assigned a different dance and then we all are assigned extra hours outside of school to work on it. I've had rehearsals all week after school and stuff but luckily, we get tomorrow off but we're rehearsing all day on Sunday.

"We don't get out until six and then I'm going over to Penn's again," Sienna explains.

After a little while longer, we all finish eating so we throw away our trash and then scatter, my friends going to find their boyfriends and me to go back to my room to watch a movie or something.

As I'm passing the fountain to get back to the dorms though, I hear somebody call out my name.

"Stella!"

I turn around even though I already know that it's Andrew and I know that I really don't want to turn around. He approaches me and I bite my tongue not to respond to him, kind of shocked that he's talking to me at all since its' been two weeks since we've had any type of contact at all and we didn't exactly end on the best of terms.

"Can we talk?" He asks me.

I shake my head at him. "I'm busy."

"Stella," He says my name and I hate how he still makes it sound like a freaking melody. "Please. Just five minutes."

I sigh and then sit down on the edge of the fountain's cement siding and then Andrew sits down beside me. "Five minutes," I remind him.

"I just wanted to know how you are. How's your wrist and everything?" He wonders and I notice how he sat uncomfortably close to me so I make it a point to dramatically get up and sit a few more inches away from him. He glances down, noticing the movement but he doesn't mention it.

"I'm fine. It's fine," I supply tersely.

"So you're still mad at me I take it?" He sighs, running his fingers through his hair.

I take a moment to study my words, to try and say the right thing but I have no idea what the right thing is right now. "I'm not mad, I just don't think that I want to talk to you right now."

"Why not?"

"You know why not," I say quietly. "Is that all that you wanted?"

He opens his mouth to speak but then closes it again as he looks down, noticing the shirt that I'm wearing today. It's a pink blouse, which is pretty average, but the thing that's special about this shirt is that the bottom button is missing. Not only missing, but it was ripped out of its threads, leaving an angry amount of little strings sticking out all over the place and even a little rip in the fabric. I know what he's thinking as he stares at the rip where the small silver button should be, because now I'm thinking about it too. And the memory still hurts so much.

"Stella," Andrew laughs as we stumble into his dorm room. We aren't drunk or anything but we stumble because we're so tangled into each other- his arms around my mid-section and my arms reaching up to his head with my fingers lacing through his dark blonde hair.

I kiss his lips and then grin at him as he fumbles to shut the door behind me. "Yes, Andrew?"

"You're beautiful," He breaths against my skin and then kisses me again, swiping his tongue across my bottom lip.

I reciprocate the passionate kiss and play those words in my head again, over and over as we're kissing with my back pressed against the wall and then his hand starts moving up my skirt. A few days ago, Andrew had told me that he loves me, when we were at the ice cream parlor, and I'm pretty sure that we're about to do it. Andrew's roommate (it was still summertime, so we still had roommates) went home for the weekend so we have the room to ourselves and I want to do it- and by the way that Andrew is feeling up my bare thigh, I'd say that he wants to as well.

His lips travel down to my neck and then he mumbles again, "You're so beautiful."

I can't hold back a small moan as I peel his shirt up and then over his head and then I glance down, enjoying the view of his abs for a moment as they rapidly cave in and then out with his quick breaths. Andrew pulls me close to him again and then carries me to the bed until I'm laying down on his twin sized mattress, looking up at the ceiling.

He starts to unbutton my blouse from the top to the bottom but his hands are shaking, so it takes longer than it normally would have. He still continues to peel away the blouse, slowly revealing my black lacy bra underneath of it and then he tugs it out from where it's tucked into my skirt. He doesn't see the last button though, and yanks the shirt open which causes the last button to rip off of the shirt and go flying to the ground with a little ping.

"Oh, shit," Andrew mumbles, looking down at the wild threads now spitting out of my shirt. "It ripped."

"It's okay, not a big deal," I pant, not wanting him to get distracted from the task at hand. I run my fingers through his hair and then he kisses me again, getting the shirt completely off of me and then throwing it to the floor. "I love you."

He smiles down at me, his hand on my bra-clad boob. "I love you too, Stell," And then he kisses me as if to prove it.

Now, that memory that used to be something amazing, something to make me grin from ear to ear, now breaks my heart more than a lot of things. I didn't even think about it when I put the blouse on this morning, I just grabbed something and slid it on over a tank top with some jeans but now, as Andrew is eyeing that ripped hole where the button used to be, I remember.

I look down at the hole and then I look over at Andrew but not his face, I look at his hands and I remember where they used to be- what they did to me that night. I press my knees together and look away, waiting for him to either speak or walk away.

"I miss that," He finally mumbles, not taking his eyes off of the hole.

I roll my eyes, trying my best to look nonchalant when in reality, I'm freaking out on the inside but I'm trying my best not to show it. "It's not that hard to get laid around here but you're asking the wrong person."

"That's not what I meant," Andrew says quickly. "Stella, I just miss being with you. I mean, yeah, I miss being with you too, but I really just miss being with you."

Before I can even stop myself from saying it, I hear myself speak, "You miss me?"

"Yes," He responds quickly. "Of course I do. I miss you like fucking crazy. These past few weeks have been hell and I don't think I can take it much longer."

"You don't act like it," I mumble, keeping my gaze down at my lap.

"Because of the Charlotte thing?" He wonders. "Stella, that was stupid. I saw you with Drew and I just lost my mind, okay? I'm sorry. I know that it's way overdue but I'm saying it now so that counts, right? I'm so sorry about everything."

"I don't want to talk about that," I shake my head.

"Don't you think that we have to though? Or we'll just keep tip toing around each other like this and it's ridiculous. We could at least be friends, right?" He offers softly.

"After everything that you've done to me, I don't think I want to be friends," I say, my voice trembling a little bit as I shuffle my feet around on the ground in the palpable awkwardness.

"Look, I know that I've messed up a lot and I want to make it up to you but I don't know how. Do you know how I can make this better?" He asks me. "That's really all that I want."

"I have to go," I say, standing up from the fountain. "I have... like, work to do and stuff."

"Stella, please," Andrew stops me from leaving by standing up as well and gently resting his hand on my shoulder so that I could have walked away, but I choose not to. Deep down, I know that I want Andrew to wear me down until I forgive him, but on the other hand, I'm still really pissed at him for everything that he's put me through.

"I miss you too," I blurt, losing a lot of my resolve by the way that his hand is squeezing my shoulder with comfort. "It's actually been driving me crazy but you've fucked up a lot. Maybe I have too, but there's just so much."

"I know," He sighs. "We can work on it though, right?"

I close my eyes tightly, running my hands over my face to try and think over everything. I think of how he treated me before we broke up, like I was always his second choice, and then I think of how he held Charlotte's hand. But then I remember all of the amazing times, before things went bad. Like how he kissed me like I was the only thing that ever mattered. And I remember how he told me that he loved me as we were eating ice cream in the parlor. How he ripped the button on my blouse. I am mad at him about all of the bad things, but I miss all of the good things too and maybe it's worth the try to attempt to fix what's wrong between us. Maybe he's really worth it. "We can try."

15 Coffee

Coffee.

It seems like such a simple word and in most conversations, it really is just such an ordinary word. But as I'm standing in front of my full length mirror, staring at the fifth outfit that I've tried on this morning, 'coffee' is driving me to the brink of insanity. I have absolutely no idea what to wear- with Andrew, I never know what to wear when we're out getting coffee, I guess.

Months ago, just as the school year starts, he texts me out of the blue on Thursday after classes and tells me that we should go get coffee with his brother, who was in town and decided to stop by. I'd met his brother once before but this time was different, because we'd had sex just a few weeks before and I feel like his brother knows that. Lucas is just four years older than Andrew and they're pretty close, which means that they tell each other almost everything and I fear that 'everything' includes what I've done with Andrew. So after class, I hurry back to my dorm and try to figure out what the hell I should wear. I always try to look nice when I'm in his family's company but I don't want to wear a dress that's too short because then his brother might think that I'm a slut or something. If I wear something too long then maybe I'm a tease. I don't know if that makes any sense, but it does to me and I'm so paranoid that Lucas won't like me. I have always really wanted his family to like me, so it's kind of a big deal but when Andrew texted me to ask me to go for coffee, I didn't let on that I was nervous, I just told him that I'd be there at five. Right now, it's 4:30 and I might have a heart attack.

Eventually, I find a dress that just barely touches my knees so it's not too short and it's not too long and there's small sleeves so I'm not too covered but there's not too much cleavage either. Being a girl is hard with all of these contradicting rules in society. Like, dresses can't be too long or too short or too tight or too baggy. Jeez. Just make up your mind. I brush my hair out and then slip on some four inch heels, which aren't too big but still fancy and tall as well.

When I finally get to the coffee place, I see Andrew's truck in the parking lot, which means that I'm last to arrive since Lucas probably drove here with Andrew. I'm right on time though, so I hurry into the large coffee shop and find Andrew and his look-alike older brother in one of the four person booths. They share almost every characteristic- their dark blonde hair, blue eyes, tall and muscular shape. However, Lucas's nose is a little bigger and his grin is a little crooked and his eye brows are a bit bushier.

"Hey," Andrew smiles when I approach the table and then he scoots over so that I can sit down beside him. "I already ordered your weird latte thing."

"Thanks," I say with a small laugh before looking over at his brother. "Hi, Lucas."

"Stella," He says with a mischievous grin. "It's so nice to see you again."

"Yeah, you too," I respond, leaning into Andrew reflexively.

And then, without any other formalities or manners, Lucas decides to cut right to the humiliating part of this trip- the part that I was terrified would happen. "So, Mom would want me to ask this. You're using protection, right? I'm too handsome to be an uncle, you know."

"Luke," Andrew snaps at his brother, shooting him a warning scowl as my face flames bright red and I look down at the table. "Seriously. Don't."

"Hey, I'm just looking out for my little bro," He laughs innocently. "You didn't think that you could hide that from me, did you? Call it brother's intuition if you will, but I can just tell."

Andrew shoots me an apologetic frown and I offer a weak smile in return. "Well, you don't need to bring it up, okay?"

"Sure," Lucas laughs again. "Anyway, Andrew, how's senior year treating you?"

And then conversation goes on as normal without any other mention of sex at all, which is a major relief because I could not feel more mortified than I did right then. I just wanted to disappear into thin air at that moment, but I just sat there and listened to the two brothers catch up since they don't see each other too often with Andrew being here and Lucas off to college at Penn State which is pretty far away so he doesn't come west too often. I'll sometimes put in a comment or two but mostly, I'm just sitting and listening and laughing at all of the right times.

After Lucas leaves to walk across the street where there's a Walmart so that he can buy a pack of Monster, Andrew turns and holds my hand in his.

"I'm sorry that my brother is kind of a jerk," He tells me apologetically. "I really didn't tell him anything."

"It's okay," I assure him with a light laugh. "He means well, I guess. Honestly, I don't care if you tell him how wickedly awesome I am in bed, I just don't want to be part of the conversation. And as long as it stays away from your parents."

Andrew grins at me, bending to kiss my lips softly. "You are wickedly awesome, Stella. In all aspects."

"Of course I am," I giggle, kissing him back but we're in public, so it's fleeting. "I have to be to keep up with your awesomeness."

He chuckles, wrapping his arm around my waist and pulling me close to him in the booth. "We're both just so incredibly awesome that we balance each other out."

"And that's exactly why we're so adorable," I decide with another small laugh.

This time, though, coffee means something else. It's not just meeting up with Lucas, it's facing a whole lot of emotions that I've bitten down for a while now. He'd texted me this morning to ask if I wanted to get coffee after practice today (somehow, we have practice at the same time, which is convenient for our purposes) and just like I always did, I texted him that I'd be there. And now, just like always, I don't know what to wear. Should it be casual or should I wear a dress? I have no idea what we're even going to talk about or how deep into the conversation we're going to get.

Finally, I decide on casual because he's seen me at my worst and my best so there's really no use in trying to impress him. I put on a pair of jeans and a gray sweater with a tiger on the front and some sneakers. I have twenty minutes to go so I start my drive to the coffee place, the same one that I went to all of those months ago with Andrew and his brother.

This time, I get there first and as I'm waiting in one of the booths for Andrew, I can feel myself getting jumpy. Is he going to show up? Is he going to be late? Am I too early? I finally see him walk through the doors and I wipe my sweaty palms on my jean-clad thighs. Here goes nothing.

I watch silently as he sits down across from me in the booth and then we order our drinks before he stares at me for a really long time and I wait for him to talk because I don't want to be the first one to speak up. I have no idea what I'd even say.

"I'm really glad that you came," Andrew tells me eventually. "I was really terrified that you wouldn't."

I swallow the dry lump in my throat. "I told you that I'd try. This is me trying," I explain.

"Right, well thank you," He says. "I don't even know where to start."

"I want to know why you did that thing with Charlotte," I say loudly, surprising both of us. "I know you said that you saw me with Drew but we were just talking- we ran into each other so we were just catching up. And you- you deliberately did that just to hurt me. And it worked- it really worked. It hurt like hell to see you with her like that and the way you looked at me. Why did you want to hurt me like that?"

He pinches his lips together and looks down to the table, obviously not expecting my outburst so soon into the conversation but I couldn't help it. I can't feed around the bush with this elephant in the room. "It sounds stupid now but I just wanted to prove to you that I was moving on too. Obviously, that wasn't true but I saw you with Drew and it just didn't feel fair that you were moving on and I wasn't. I know that's not what was actually happening with you but it just felt that way and... I don't know. I didn't mean to hurt you, Stella, I just wanted to make a point. I know that it was stupid- I've been acting pretty stupid for a while but I think I've finally gotten it together. I'm so sorry, Stella. About everything. I want to make everything right but I just don't know how."

"That's insane," I mumble.

"You make me insane, Stella," He tells me. "When I stopped by the ice cream shop, I was on my way to buy you flowers. You know those spikey purple ones with the curly leaves?"

"Phacelia," I remember the flower that he's describing and I remember all of those weird flowers that he's found and brought to me and then I can't hold back a small laugh.

"Yeah, those. Well, I didn't buy them obviously but the point is that I want you back. I've wanted you back since the day you ended things, actually, but I just have a stupid, weird way of trying to prove it," Andrew explains.

"Why'd it take me breaking up with you for you to realize that you still like me?" I wonder quietly.

Andrew looks up at me, frowning in confusion. "Stella, I've always loved you. I never thought otherwise. Why would you think that?"

"Because that's how you acted," I tell him. "You ignored me all of the time, you'd always turn me down when I invited you places, you'd snap at me for no reason, even when I was standing right beside you, you'd act like you could care less about me. You made me feel like shit, Andrew."

"I... I didn't mean to," He mumbles slowly. "I didn't think that it affected you that much. I was just so caught up in the game that I didn't even realize that you were bothered by it."

"Well, it was killing me," I croak, looking down at my lap. "And you should have seen that."

"I know," Andrew sighs. "I know that I should have. I took you for granted way too much and I'm sorry, Stella. I'm going to make it up to you somehow."

I shake my head and wipe a premature tear from my right eye. "Andrew..." I trail off, having no idea what I should say anymore. Having no idea how I should feel.

"I mean it," He tells me with a nod. "I love you, Stella. I love you so much and these past few weeks have been absolutely hell without you. And even though I know that you're incredibly pissed at me, I know that you haven't been all that well off either. You miss me too, right? Even after everything I've done, I know that you miss me."

"I miss the old you," I snap. "I miss the guy who liked to buy me weird flowers and ordered my drinks for me. Not the guy who ignores me like I'm nothing and tries to make me jealous."

"I'm not like that. I realize now that how I treated you was terrible and I know that I made a lot of mistakes and I'm really sorry about it all."

I start to hide my face in my hands, unsure of what I should say or think anymore. Should I forgive him? Should I never talk to him again? I have no idea what I'm going to do or what I should say or feel or think. The only thing I can feel myself feeling is overwhelmed. Overwhelmed with confusion between my head and my heart and common sense and Andrew. "I'm so tired of getting hurt," I mumble with a sniffle and I don't even bother trying to wipe the tears that are running down my face.

Andrew reaches over the table and catches one of my hands in his, squeezing tightly. "I'm not going to hurt you again. I swear."

"You've already broken that promise before," I remind him coldly, angrily pulling my hand from his grip.

"I know," He sighs. "But it'll be different now, okay?"

I suddenly realize that sitting here just hurts too much now. Hearing his voice, feeling his hand squeeze mine protectively, it all just hurts so much and I feel like if I don't leave right now, I'm going to lose it. I don't want to be here anymore. I don't want to have to think about this or Andrew or forgiveness or change. My head hurts, my eyes burn, my hands are trembling, and my knees are weak.

"Stell, please don't leave," Andrew says quickly as I stand up from the booth and grab my latte.

"It sucks, doesn't it?" I wonder rhetorically, still really mad at him for everything that he's done and now he's asking me for forgiveness and I'm so glad that he is, I really am, but I'm also still really mad at him and I want him to know that. "Being the one left behind."

And then I leave and I don't look back, but I do sit in my car and cry for an embarrassingly long amount of time before driving back to campus to try and decide what the hell that I'm going to do.

If this chapter gets 144 votes and 34 comments then I'll post the teaser for Cry Until You Bleed (:

Thanks so much for reading! You're all beautiful <3

16 Holiday Plans

"I'm sorry, honey, but we won't be able to make it," My mom tells me apologetically over the phone.

I sigh and roll my eyes, trying to remain calm even though she's seriously driving me crazy right now. "You already missed it, Mom. The show ended an hour ago."

"Oh," She mumbles slowly. "Crap. I forgot about the time difference."

"Yeah, it doesn't matter. You wouldn't have made it anyway," I remind her as I'm sitting outside of the ballroom, in the lobby of the Arena in my red Christmas dance dress and low lace black heels. After the show, there's an after party in the ballroom since both the auditorium and the ballroom are both in the big Arena so we have the Christmas show in the auditorium and then the after party in the ballroom, which is what's going on right now. My parents said that they'd be here but they obviously didn't show up, which is why I came out to the quiet lobby to call my mom.

"I really am so sorry, dear. We just got caught up with this project in Chicago for the homeless," She explains apologetically. "I bet you were amazing though."

"Yeah," I sigh. "Well, you're coming to visit for Christmas, right? Or I can fly to Chicago or wherever you are. I'm sure Anthony will come too, actually."

"Stella," My mom sighs in that way that I know that she's about to shoot down my idea.

"Right, I understand," I assure her, trying not to sound as disappointed as I actually was. "It's just that Christmas is usually the only sure fire holiday that we get to see you guys."

"Yeah, but we saw each other for Thanksgiving which was only a month ago, so it'll be fine, right?" She wonders as if it's normal for a child to see her parents less than once a month. I spent my visit on a shitty Thanksgiving so I don't get a Christmas visit too. That'd be crazy talk.

"Yeah, that totally makes sense. Awesome," I mutter and I know that she won't hear the sarcasm in my voice because she's always been terrible at detecting my wonderful sense of sarcasm. I'm sitting down on a bench against the wall of the lobby and I'm leaning forward with my elbows resting on my knees, trying to keep it together.

Ever since my talk with Andrew about a week ago, I've been finding it harder and harder to just keep myself together and this conversation with my mom isn't making anything any better. I haven't talked to Andrew in the week that has gone by since we had coffee but when I pass him in the hallways and at lunch, he smiles at me. I can't find it in myself to smile back but I offer him a wave in return.

"Maybe we can make it up for spring break or something. We'll work something out," My mom assures me as if spring break isn't months and months away. I know that my parents are really distant but for some reason, I still find comfort in seeing them in person. Our Christmases are really the best part of the year in terms of my parents because we'll spend all day together, just the four of us, and they'll give us presents and we'll give them something too even though we use their money to buy it. It's the thought, right? We'll have dinner together and everything and it's just an amazing holiday for our family. Apparently, it doesn't mean as much to them as it does to me though.

"Sure, Mom," I inform her, trying not to sound deflated. That's basically the only way that I talk to her- always attempting to mask how I really feel. What's the point in emotions when they have better things to worry about? She has the ability to just brush off any type of sentimental talk and then end the conversation. That's just how she is, so I've learned to just mask anything that I'm feeling. "Well, I'll let you get back to your homeless people. You're probably pretty busy over there."

"We've been pretty slow for the past few days," She tells me and that just makes me want to scream at her. If she was so slow with the homeless people, why couldn't they just make a day out of it and fly over here to see the show? Why is that so hard to do?

"Right, well I'll talk to you later then," I say quickly, not really wanting to talk to her anymore and I also don't want to her to hear me cry, which is about to happen, I'm pretty sure.

"Goodbye, sweetheart," My mom says with a loud sigh just before hanging up the phone and then my phone beeps, letting me know that the phone call has ended and I am now completely alone. Putting my phone back into my purse, I run my fingers through my hair and then hide my face behind my palms as I try to breathe. Maybe if my breathing is steady and long then I can hold myself together. The secret is through the breathing.

"Hey," I hear Andrew's voice as he walks into the lobby from the ballroom. "You don't look like you're at a party."

I remove my hands from my face and look at him as he walks closer to me but I don't respond to him.

He sits down beside me and slightly nudges me with his shoulder. "Come on, Stell. What's wrong?"

"Nothing," I say with a small shake of my head. "I'm just fine."

"Stella," He says my name again, obviously unconvinced. "You can talk to me, you know. I'm sure that you don't want to, but I'm just saying that you can if you want to. I'm right here."

"It's just that my parents aren't coming for Christmas," I find myself telling him before I can even stop myself. It's just so easy to talk to him, the words just unwillingly flow out of me like ugly vomit. "I guess it's whatever."

"Wow, that really sucks," He tells me and that's one of the things that I love about talking to Andrew about things like this. He doesn't sugar coat the reality of the situation by telling me that 'it's not so bad' or that 'it'll all work out' but he helps me get through it with honesty. "But you know that they love you, they just show it differently than most people."

"Right," I sigh. "I know."

"I mean, if you want an awesome Christmas then you can come with me to New Mexico for winter break. You know how my mom is with the holiday thing."

"Andrew," I mumble hesitantly, running my fingers through my hair as I look down at my feet, not really knowing what to say. Of course I have to say no to his offer- it'd be ridiculous to even consider agreeing with him.

"Look, I know that you probably think that it's an insane idea but it's just an offer. You deserve a real Christmas if that's what you want, you know? I want to give you everything you want and this is the best that I can do.

I didn't tell my mom about us yet so she's probably already expecting you to come anyway."

"I can't do that. It'd be weird," I say, shaking my head again.

"I mean, we were friends before, right? We can go back to that- or at least maybe try? It has to be better than this avoiding each other thing that's been going on for the past few weeks."

Pursing my lips, I glance over at him, up at the ceiling, and then back over to Andrew. "I have to make sure that Anthony has something to do. If not, I'm not going to let him spend Christmas alone."

"So if he's fine then it's a yes?" He wonders hopefully.

I nod because he's right- being friends with him is a lot better than nothing at all. I'd been mad at him for a long time for how he had treated me and for the Charlotte thing that now feels like it was years ago. Of course, I will not just forget about all of that stuff, but I can agree to get over it and at least be friends with him. It'll hurt like hell to be around him more than I am now and not be able to kiss him or hold his hand or anything like that, but it'll still hurt less than not being around him at all.

He grins, looking about as excited as a little kid who just saw Santa, and his grin is just so wide that I can't help but smile back a little bit. But if we're friends, I realize, I can't smile at his smile like I want to- like I'm used to. We'll be friends but that's it. For now, I think. We just have a lot to figure out, I guess, and jumping back into a relationship without figuring everything out is just a really bad idea. "That's awesome. I actually have to buy my plane ticket tonight so I'll get one for you too then, yes?"

"Let me talk to Anthony first," I say softly and then I stand up from the bench that we're sharing. "I'll let you know, okay?"

"Yeah, sure," He says, standing up from the bench as well and as I turn to walk away, he grabs my hand before I can really leave. "Stella, you're really considering this? Coming to Christmas with me and everything. I really didn't think that you'd be up for it."

I nod in all honesty because yes, I really am considering it. I'm not so sure if I will talk myself into it or not, but I'm definitely thinking about it. It seems like something that could really help me calm down, stop freaking out over every small thing in my life like a pregnant lady. "Yeah, I swear."

He offers me a small smile, nods, and then I walk away to go find my brother.

I find him talking to a group of guys that I know from school but I don't really talk to any of them. When Anthony sees me approaching, he offers me a small smile.

"Hey, Stell. What's up?" He wonders.

I open my mouth to speak but I'm not so sure what I want him to say. Do I want him to have plans so that I can go with Andrew or do I want him to say that he's free and then I'll stay here with him? I have no idea which way I want this to go but the fact that no matter what, it's out of my hands gives me a piece of mind in some way. No matter what I want, it's either going one way or another. "I was just wondering what you're doing for Christmas? Since Mom and Dad are in Chicago and everything."

"Mom and Dad are in Chicago?" He wonders curiously.

I nod. "Just got off of the phone with Mom. Christmas is a no-go. So do you have any plans?"

"Uh, I don't think so…" He trails off and my heart starts pounding in my chest but I'm not sure if it's disappointment or relief.

"Dude, we're going skiing over in Jackson Hole," One of his friends interrupts the conversation. "You should come with us. Their New Year party is insane."

Anthony acknowledges the invitation and then looks over at me. "Is that okay with you? Or do you want to go do something?"

"No, that's totally fine," I say quickly, feeling a smile spread across my face and it's in that moment that what I feel right now is relief that I don't have to stay here with my brother. I mean, I love him and all but I think I'd actually rather be in New Mexico with Andrew. "I have a thing to do."

"Of course, you are always welcome to come with us too, Stella," One of his other friends, his name is Ashton, I think, grins at me.

I offer the guy a sarcastic smile. "Thanks. I'm going to pass though- I have my own holiday plans. Merry Christmas, Anthony."

"Yeah, you too, Stell," He says as I'm walking away from the group, still with a smile on my face. Before I can start looking for Andrew, he appears right in front of me.

"You're smiling," He observes. "But I don't know if that means that you can't go or you can."

"Anthony's going skiing in Wyoming," I inform him, trying to bite down my smile, but I don't think I do a very good job. "So I can come with you. If it's okay with your mom and everything."

He grins even wider than before and then, in return, I'm smiling a little bit as well. "Have you met my mom? Of course she's okay with you coming. She loves you."

"Okay. Um, thanks for doing this, Andrew," I mutter softly. "But I don't want it to be weird. How can we spend two weeks together without it being weird?"

"It won't be weird," He assures me. "I promise. Like I said before, we've been friends for years so we can do it again, even after everything that's happened."

Just friends. Somehow, I'm thinking that the idea is impossible when it comes to me and Andrew. Friends aren't supposed to feel like this towards other friends. Loving his smile, hating his tendencies and obliviousness. Everything that I feel towards Andrew, I feel so passionately that I know that no matter what happens in the future, we will never be able to just be friends again. We both know it, but we're both in a state of denial right now in order to be around each other without being with each other. So we'll ignore the inevitable just for now and hope that it'll work out which is probably a bad idea but right now, it feels fine to me. "When are we going to leave then?"

"Uh, either Sunday or Monday," He says. "I'll text you later tonight with the flight time."

"Okay," I say quietly, feeling uncharacteristically shy at the moment and I'm not so sure why. "Well, I'm going to go find Sienna and Mason. I'll… I'll talk to you soon, Andrew."

"Right, yeah, I'll see you soon," He agrees as I offer him an awkward goodbye wave and then turn and walk away, trying to stay stable on my shaky knees.

I find Sienna talking to her boyfriend, Penn, in the corner of the busy ballroom of people excited for both the awesomely executed show and the two week break that we're now free for.

"Good show, Stella," Penn compliments me as I approach them.

I offer him a smile and then I say, "I guess I learned from the best," I joke, referring to the time over the summer when he was my dance instructor.

Sienna rolls her eyes and gently shoves her boyfriend's buff shoulder. "Please do not inflate his ego. He really doesn't need it."

He scoffs and looks over at her. "You love my ego."

He turns to kiss her but she puts her hand to his mouth, intercepting the kiss, and then she turns to me and changes the subject. "Hey, what was that about with Andrew?" She wonders.

"He invited me to go to New Mexico with him for break," I inform her, offering Penn a small hello wave that he politely returns. "Because my parents bailed."

Her eyes widen a little bit- at which part of my explanation, I do not know- and then she says, "Wow, really? What did you tell him?"

"After talking to Anthony, I told him yes. I mean, we can just be friends, right?"

"So you're going to take the 'just friends' approach?" She wonders. "Are you sure that's going to work?"

"No," I shake my head. "I'm actually pretty positive that it won't work but I don't care. I'm just going to take it day by day for right now."

"Okay then. Whatever you say. I'm just glad that you two aren't avoiding each other anymore because that was awful," Sienna says. "And as long as you're happy, then I say go for it."

"Yeah, I'm not so sure what's happy anymore," I sigh. "But it's worth a shot, I guess. Anyway, I think I'm going to head back to the dorms. I'm pretty drained. If you see Mason, tell her that I'll see her tomorrow."

"Sure, okay. See you tomorrow," Sienna says with a small smile. I decide that I'll explain everything to her and Mason at the same time- how I'm going to New Mexico, how I feel about it, how I'm so confused about everything- and I also figure that Penn probably doesn't want to hear about my girl problems either. I offer them both a wave again and then walk away, back into the crowd, to find the door that leads into the lobby.

When I finally walk through to the lobby, I hear two familiar voices going back and forth on the other side of one of the pillars in the lobby.

"I'm just saying that what you're trying to do is ridiculous, Charlotte. And it's so pathetic," I hear somebody say. It's strange though, because it sounds like Charlotte but unless she's talking to herself, I'd say it's probably not her. Then I remember that she has a twin but I barely ever even talk to Heather that it took me a minute to remember that she exists. To be honest, I don't even know if she's as awful as Charlotte- or awful at all- because I've never spoken to her.

"Oh, come on. Don't be such a wuss. I'm just having a little bit of fun, okay?"

"No," Heather snaps. "It's ridiculous, you trying to get in the middle of a relationship like this. Don't you think that you've done enough?"

Suddenly, it occurs to me that they might be talking about me and Andrew. Instead of walking past them like I need to do to get to the door, I just stand there, hidden by another pillar, to listen to the conversation just because I'm that nosy.

"Heather, you worry too much. Everything is fine," Charlotte assures her twin.

"It's not fine," She argues. "You are just trying to cause drama- just like you did back home- and it needs to stop before you get yourself into some serious trouble. Leave Andrew and Stella alone. Let them figure everything out without you trying to make things worse."

And that proves my theory right, so I keep listening.

"Look, all I'm going to do is invite him to the New Year resort with us- that's it. If he doesn't take the bait then I'll accept that he's just not into me and I'll move on, okay?" Charlotte negotiates.

"He's already made it pretty clear that he's really not into you. Why do you have to keep trying?" Heather seems exhausted and honestly, if I was Charlotte's sister, I'd be exhausted with dealing with her too.

I decide that I like Heather- at least, she's a lot better than her devil counterpart. I also decide that I don't feel like overhearing anymore of their conversation, so I leave the pillar that I'm standing behind and start walking towards the exit of the building. My heels clack against the tile of the lobby, which makes both twins go silent as they turn to look at me but I ignore them, pretending like I don't even notice them at all as I leave the building.

I force myself not to think about what I heard Charlotte saying, how she's trying to get Andrew to spend the New Year with him, because I think that if I even thought about it, it'd give me a panic attack or something. What if he does take the bait and decide to leave his family's house early to go with her? What if he decides to not let me come with him to New Mexico just so that he can go with Charlotte to wherever it is that she's going?

So I don't even think about it after I get to my dorm, I just lay down, watch a movie, and hope for the best.

17 Second Guessing

"I'm not so sure about this anymore," I choke out as I'm standing in the terminal with my carry on hanging in the crook of my elbow and Andrew's standing across from me.

He frowns a little bit. "You don't want to come anymore? Why not?"

"Because..." I trail off, looking down at my shoes. My heart is pounding in my chest with nerves as I continue to second guess my decision to tag along on Andrew's trip to New Mexico to see his family. My knees are wobbly, my palms are clammy, my forehead is covered in a thin layer of damp sweat. "It's such a bad idea. We... we can't do this. What were we even thinking?"

"We were thinking that it'd be nice to spend some time together- to be able to talk things out- and to be friends again," He reminds me. "It'll be fine, Stella. I promise."

"Because your promise means so much?" I snap at him. He starts to chew on his bottom lip and looks down to the ugly carpet below our feet, looking a little embarrassed. "I-I'm sorry. That was mean but I'm just saying that we can't be together like this without something happening. Not anymore."

"So then let something happen," He says, putting a hand on my shoulder to keep me from walking away, which I'm not going to do yet but I can tell that he's afraid that I will.

"But what if it's not a good thing? The thing about us is that we're passionate about each other. Everything that we feel, it's passionate. Whether that be love or anger. So this trip could either go terribly wrong or really awesome and I'm really afraid that it's going to be the former."

"It doesn't have to be though," Andrew assures me. "Come on, Stell. Give it a chance, okay? You never know."

Over the intercom, the lady announces that they're ready to start boarding for our flight and my knees become even more wobbly. I could just walk away- just pay Andrew back for the plane ticket and catch a cab back to the school where I can spend two weeks hanging out with Mason and Sienna and Brian, who all have family here in California and don't need to go anywhere for their holidays. I don't have to do this. However, even as I think all of these things, I still find myself walking towards the gate, getting in line with everybody else on their way to ABQ.

"This will be good for us, you'll see," Andrew tells me, putting his hand on my shoulder again and squeezing a little bit for comfort.

"I just don't want to fight," I mutter under my breath. "I'm so tired of fighting."

"I know. Me too," He agrees. The line starts moving at a rapid pace and then suddenly, we're that the front so I hand the lady my ticket, she scans it, and then I walk past her, into the little hall thing that leads us into the plane. I think that Andrew switched our tickets on purpose because my ticket says Andrew Haggerty on it and his has my name on it. I wondered why he did that as we were sitting in the terminal but now, as we're on the plane, I realize that his seat is a window seat and he knows how much I love windows.

A smile tugs at the corners of my lips as I slide into the seat and Andrew sits beside me. It's a small plane, so there's only two seats on each side of the plane which means that he doesn't have to sit next to any strangers, which is nice because that's always awkward.

"So," I say after about a ten minute silence as everybody files into the plane. "Can I ask you something?"

"You can ask me anything," He assures me and I notice how he's resting his hand on the armrest with his palm up like an invitation for me to hold it, but I don't. "What is it?"

"Have you talked to Charlotte lately?" I ask him, remembering the conversation that I overheard from her and her sister a few days ago at the after party.

"Charlotte? No, I haven't. Why?"

"I just heard her talking about inviting you to this thing," I explain quietly.

"Oh, the New Year's thing?" He wonders, looking over at me. I look over at him too but I don't look up at his face, I just keep steady eye contact with his shoulder so that I don't let his blue eyes turn me into goo like they do so easily all of the time.

"So she did talk to you about it?"

"No, Heather did. Well, she told me that Charlotte was trying to talk to me about it so I just avoided her all day yesterday so that she couldn't ask me."

"Oh," I mumble. "Would you have said no if she did ask you?"

"Of course I would have, Stella," Andrew says with a little incredulous laugh. "It's just a lot easier not having to say no- you know how I suck at that kind of stuff- so I just kind of avoided her."

"She's such a gross person," I mumble. "I really hate her."

"I know you do," He nods and I prepare to hear him defend her again like he always used to when we were together, telling me that she's actually pretty cool or not that bad. But then, he surprises me by saying, "She really is a pain in the ass."

"Really," I sigh, glancing up at him. "I thought you liked her."

"I don't. I mean, at first, I thought she was okay but after a while, she just started getting on my nerves. And then I just realized that she wasn't ever an okay person, she's just really manipulative and you were right all along."

I snort and turn to look out the window. "Obviously."

"Well, you know how I am. I like to give people the benefit of the doubt," He explains. "And it just took me a bit too long to realize how awful she is and I'm sorry."

I don't respond to him at first, I just process his words. Let them sink in. I think for a while and Andrew doesn't interrupt me from my thoughts while we both silently watch the plane start to back away from the building and then start to move towards the runway for takeoff.

I watch like an eager child as the plane's wings start to flap and then the plane begins to shoot down the runway like a mean bullet until we're tilting into the air, letting go of the road beneath us to soar into the air for another place to land. Once we're steady in the air and the show is over, I lean back in my chair and glance over at Andrew.

"Thanks for giving me the window," I say in a small voice.

"You're welcome," He says back, his voice almost as small as mine, as if we're both afraid to speak right now- to say the wrong thing.

"I want to know if you cheated on me," I blurt, deciding that it's ridiculous to be afraid of that. How are we going to figure anything out if we're just tiptoeing around each other's feelings like little baby birds afraid of being squashed? Nothing is going to be easier if we avoid the hard topics, it'll just lead to more awkwardness.

"Cheated on you?" Andrew wonders incredulously, as if I just asked him if he has three arms or something. "Stella, are you serious?"

"Why are you so surprised?" I ask him in return. "You took a liking to Charlotte, you felt really guilty about when you hung out with her and then you lied about it. Why is that such a surprising thing for me to ask? Because you were boyfriend of the year or something?"

"Okay, fine," He concedes. "I guess I can understand where you're coming from but no, I never cheated on you. I never wanted to either. I was just trying to be nice to her."

"Did you guys hook up after we broke up then?" I ask, turning to look out the window again as we fly through the clouds and then over them.

"No," He tells me. "The closest I ever got to Charlotte was holding her hand that one day just to make you mad. That's really all and it obviously wasn't even real. Stella, I swear."

"That was so mean," I nearly whisper as I remember that day and that gut wrenching glare aimed right at me as he latched onto her hand. I remember how empty I felt too.

"I know," He mutters.

"It really killed me," I say. "I mean, after everything that'd happened, I didn't think it was possible to feel even worse but seeing you like that... it was the worst out of everything."

"And I'm so sorry about it," He insists. "I completely overreacted about seeing you with Drew and I'm so sorry that I'm a complete idiot. I really am."

"I know you are," I tell him. "I mean, I know that you're sorry, not that you're an idiot. Even though come to think of it, you are pretty idiotic as well."

"Funny," He jokes sarcastically. "Seriously though, I really want to make things right between us."

I close my eyes. "How?"

"I have no idea, but I'll figure something out."

"Why did I have to break up with you before you realized that you still cared about me?" I ask him softly, looking out the window now instead of looking up at Andrew.

"I've always cared, Stella," He assures me.

"Well, you didn't act like it at all. I tried so hard to be the best I could be for you- I was always there, trying to spend time with you but trying not to be smothering. I always invited you everywhere and I tried... I just tried so hard but you just stopped trying. Everything that you did, it was either ignoring me or doing something to deliberately hurt me. That's all you ever did. It made me feel like shit all of the time."

"I didn't mean to be like that, I was just so caught up in everything that I didn't realize that I was hurting you like that," He explains apologetically.

"But when you broke up with me, it was like a wakeup call for me but every time that I tried to make things better, everything just got worse."

I wipe a tear off of my cheek even though I'm not even sure why I'm crying. I should be happy about being here with Andrew, trying to fix everything between us, and I am happy. I'm also really overwhelmed and that results in tears. Ugly, nonstop tears.

"Stell, I didn't mean to make you cry. I'm sorry," He says quietly, placing a hand on my shoulder as if he wants to comfort me but he doesn't know how without crossing a line.

"No, it's fine," I assure him with a small sniffle. "It's just that... I actually don't know why I'm crying."

He doesn't say anything after that, he just reaches behind me, wrapping his arm behind my back and pulling me into his side while simultaneously lifting up the armrest so that there's nothing between us. We just sit there like that for the rest of the plane ride. Even after my uncalled for tears, I just lay into his side, take in his familiar smell, and enjoy the moment because I'm sure that it's fleeting. After we land in New Mexico, I have no idea what's going to happen so I need to hold on to this moment for as long as I can until it's gone.

When the plane ends, we walk quietly to the baggage claim and then towards the passenger pickup zone where Lucas is going to pick us up since both of Andrew's parents are still at work but this is their last day of work until Christmas is over.

"Does Lucas know anything about us?" I ask Andrew as we're walking with our luggage towards the rows of cars that are picking people up from the airport. There's a couple reuniting just a few cars in front of us, hugging and crying and kissing. To my left, there's a family that's greeting back an older woman who might be their mother from what looks like a business trip.

"Yeah, he knows," He assures me. "When I went home for Thanksgiving, I just told my parents that we were fighting but I didn't actually tell them that we were broken up. Lucas could tell though."

"He'll probably hate me then," I mumble, feeling (once again) that coming along on this trip was such a terrible idea. We need time to talk and think things over instead of just going face first into a two week long vacation together with his family. Including Lucas, who is very protective of his little brother when he needs to be.

"He doesn't hate you, Stell," Andrew assures me.

"Andrew, I-"

"It'll be fine," He interrupts me. "I promise, just relax. Everything will work out."

"I'm trying to relax but this was just such a bad idea," I mumble.

"Maybe but you're already here so you might as well just be optimistic about it, okay? It could really work out."

"I know," I sigh, seeing a red car pull up and Lucas pop his head out the window with a wide grin, probably excited to see his brother again. I think the last time they saw each other was Thanksgiving which was about a month ago and that's really saying something since these two are really close.

As Lucas got out of the car to help us with our bags, I take a deep breath. Here we go. Here goes nothing.

If you haven't read it yet, the teaser for Cry Until You Bleed is posted!

Also, I'm about 50k away from getting a million votes altogether and I'd be so happy if that happened so I'd really appreciate it if you super-vote and just vote and vote and also comment because I love hearing all of your opinions.

Okay, love you guys! Thanks for reading! <3

18 Mixed Emotions

"Stella! It has been way too long," Andrew's mother is saying as she wraps me in a tight hug once she arrives at the house after work, only about ten minutes after we had gotten back to the house. After leaving the airport, we stopped at a restaurant to eat and we stayed there for a few hours just talking to Lucas. It was awkward at first (only for me) but after a while, I realized that Andrew was right- Lucas didn't seem to hold anything against me at all. He didn't even talk about the breakup at all, as if he didn't even know about it but I could tell by the curious looks he was giving Andrew that he did know, he was just being polite by saying nothing.

"Yeah," I agree with his mom, hugging her back. "Hi, Marie. It's nice to see you."

"We have so much catching up to do. We missed you at Thanksgiving," She says, stepping back and grinning at me excitedly. Andrew and Lucas are outside playing basketball but I came in to get something to drink when I saw Marie pull up so she hasn't even seen Andrew yet so I figure that I should go get him so that they can say their hellos.

"My family actually had Thanksgiving this year," I say without telling her that even if my family didn't have a Thanksgiving because at the time, the breakup was pretty recent and the wounds were still fresh so I most definitely wouldn't have been here with Andrew anyway.

"Well, that's lovely," She grins at me. "Let me go get settled and go find Andrew and then we'll really start talking."

"Sure. I'll go tell Andrew that you're home," I inform her as I start for the door. Just as I'm about to step outside, both Andrew and Lucas walk through the door before I can even get it open. They reek of sweat from all of the basketball they've been playing so I kind of feel sorry for Marie when Andrew rushes over to her and engulfs her in a sweaty hug.

"Hey, Ma," He greets her.

"You could have waited until you didn't stink so bad," She mumbles with a small laugh as she hugs him back. "You stink, Andrew. But how have you been? How's school?"

"I've been... good," He says and I wonder if she can tell that he's lying by the way that he chokes on the word 'good'. I awkwardly shuffle my feet and look down at the floor and listen to the rest of their conversation as I stand off to the side, waiting for Marie to leave the room.

"What do we do now?" I ask Andrew when we're eventually standing in the kitchen by ourselves since his mom went to put all of her work stuff away and Lucas went... I don't know where he went but he left the kitchen with his mother, leaving me and Andrew alone. It's kind of awkward, being here with Andrew, especially since his mother doesn't know that we're not actually together and his brother does and it's all kind of complicated.

Andrew shrugs. "I don't know. What do you want to do? We can watch a movie or something before my mom will want to take us out to dinner."

"I think that you should tell her," I say quickly before I can even register what's coming out of my mouth. "About us."

He burrows his eyebrows in confusion. "Why?"

"Because..." I trail off, trying to find something in my muddled brain to say to him right now. "It's so awkward, her thinking that we're together and everything. It's just weird that she thinks that we're still dating when we're not. And I'm terrible at keeping secrets. I also feel terrible that I'm kind of lying to your mom when she's such a nice person. I can't do that. You have to tell her. I mean, what if she buys us matching sweaters for Christmas or something?"

"Stella, slow down. Nobody's getting matching sweaters, okay?" Andrew tells me. "Look, I'll tell her. Just give it a few days, let's get settled in a little bit and then I'll tell her."

"Do you think that she'd hate me?" I wonder hesitantly, wondering how Marie or Andrew's father would react if they found out that me and Andrew are broken up but I'm still here for their Christmas celebration.

"Come on, you know that she won't hate you. She loves you. Not just as my girlfriend, she loves you as a person too. She'll be fine with it but I still just don't want to tell her yet. Just a few days, okay?"

"Fine," I sigh, leaning against the counter behind me. "Thanks."

"Of course. Now, do you want to go watch a movie or something?" Andrew offers. "I still have that weird one with the talking horse that you love."

"I do love that movie," I agree, following Andrew out of the kitchen and then into the living room. When he starts to go for the stairs though, I stop him. "Wait, where are you going? Aren't we going to watch it down here?"

"Um. Well, I thought we could just watch it in my room. So we won't get interrupted or anything," He explains with a small shrug.

"It's not like we're going to be doing anything that can be interrupted," I say, blinking slowly a few times. "We're just watching a movie."

"Right but you know how loud my brother can be," He tells me. "Look, Stella, I'm not trying to lure you into some kind of diabolical plan to make out with you or anything. You know me better than that. It's just a movie."

"Okay. You're right, I know. It's fine," I say, shaking my head a little bit as I follow him up the stairs and then down the hallway and into his old room. He hasn't really redecorated since he left for school after 8th grade so everything is pretty childish, including the tiny twin sized bed in the corner and the Batman stickers that cover his dresser. The stickers though, bring back a memory I've suddenly felt pop into my head about the first (and last) time that I'd traveled to Andrew's home and saw his room.

I was so upset when I found out that he was a DC fan but then he explained to me that it was just a phase when he was twelve. He couldn't just get a new dresser just because he had a DC phase. And then he continued to explain that the DC comics are actually pretty good, it's just the movies that aren't top notch. I mean, the Batman movies are okay but Marvel is better with the movies hands down.

"I can't believe you still have that dresser," I tell Andrew, looking at all of the Batman stickers that are now fading and beginning to peel off. "It's so despicable."

He laughs and walks around me, heading for the TV and the DVD stand. "I know that you're a diehard Marvel fan but DC really isn't that bad."

"Despicable," I repeat stubbornly as I sit on the corner of his small bed and wait for him to put the movie into his DVD player and starts the movie. "We should have made popcorn while we were downstairs."

"We should have," He agrees, sitting down beside me, but not too close and I'm sure he is careful not to sit too close. "But we'll have dinner in a few hours so I'm sure we'll survive."

"Yeah, I guess so," I sigh dramatically. "When's the last time that you saw this movie?"

"Since the last time that we watched it," He tells me. "Remember? When we went to the ordered pizza from the place that puts macaroni on their pizza? And the delivery guy hit on you."

"He didn't hit on me," I say with a small laugh as I remember the night as well. "He was just friendly and you were just jealous."

"He was hitting on you," Andrew insists. "But anyway, that's the last time that I watched the movie."

"Okay, well I guess that's probably because I basically have to force you to watch it. I don't get how you don't like this movie. Seriously."

He laughs a little bit. "I don't know. It's okay, I guess."

"It is more than okay. It's amazing and yet, the only reason that you have it here is to let me talk you into watching it so that you can later talk me into something else," I explain. "When in reality, you should have this movie purely on the basis of how awesome it is."

"Do you realize that by trying to talk me into loving this movie, you're talking through the movie?" He counters with an amused smile.

"Do you realize that I will never not defend this movie whenever we watch it?" I mimic his question. "I've seen it a billion times- I can talk over it and still know exactly what's going on. For example, he's about to ask her to the fake dance but she's going to reject him because she's a total bitch."

"You're so beautiful when you're passionate," I hear him say quietly, almost a whisper in the breeze that I can barely hear.

I feel a shiver crawl up my spine with that sentence and I turn my attention back to the movie before frowning and clearing my throat. "You can't say stuff like that," I mutter softly.

"I know," He mumbles.

"Especially not right now," I add, turning back to look at him but looking angry this time.

"I'm sorry," Andrew tells me and then clears his throat. "I'll, uh, go make that popcorn."

"No," I quickly. "You can't just say something like that and then leave."

"Well then what do you want me to do?" He asks me.

"I don't know," I sigh. "But you can't make this weird."

"I'm not trying to," He insists. "But I just... it's hard."

"You know that we're not going to be able to watch this movie without things being awkward," I say, leaning forward with my elbows resting on my knees. "We should... I don't know, talk about things. Set boundaries and stuff."

"Did you get that out of a women's health magazine?" Andrew jokes with a humorless laugh.

I give him a look. "It sounds kind of stupid, I know, but I can't take two weeks of you saying things like that and making it weird between us again. And here's a random question but where am I going to sleep?" I ask him because when I think about it, I realize that every other time that I'd stayed here, I'd sleep in here with Andrew but now, I think that'd add even more to the weirdness of our relationship and I don't think we need to add anymore weirdness.

"You can sleep in here. I'll take the couch downstairs or pull out an extra mattress from the attic or something," He shrugs. "Is that really the biggest problem that you can think of right now?"

"No. There's also those small compliments under your breath and the way that you look at me sometimes. You look at me like... like you love me or something."

"Well, I do love you," He reminds me.

"Stop acting like it though," I snap at him. "I can't take it, okay?"

"Alright."

"I'm really going to try and give this a chance, Andrew, but it's hard for me too," I tell him. "To hear you say this stuff and to see you look at me like that- I just want to go back to the way that things were before everything happened."

"Things can go back- maybe not exactly like they were, but we can still fix whatever broke between us. We're not a lost cause. Not yet," Andrew tells me. "I'm trying to stop it with the comments but I'll never stop looking at you like that. I can't. I can't not love you and I can't pretend like I don't. I'm sorry but you know that I've never been a good actor."

"You're driving me insane, you know," I mumble, wondering how it's even possible to feel so conflicted about wanting to be with somebody so much while simultaneously wanting to stay mad at them- to remember all of the crap that he's pulled lately. But that first part of me seems to be winning me over even more by the second. I remember all of the good times at the beginning of our relationship- all of the laughing, the kissing, the happiness. I remember it all and I just want to go back.

"The feeling's mutual," He counters softly. The tone of voice that he's using now, the dark husky undertone, it makes my heart both stop and beat faster at the same time. I feel like I'm the only person that ever hears this part of him- a piece of him that is only mine. It belongs to me.

"Do…" I trail off, my words getting choked up in my throat because I know that I shouldn't be letting him get to me this way but I also know that I can't help it. "Do you want to kiss me?" After I choke out the question, I realize how stupid I sound and I start to blush and look away from him, waiting for him to laugh or respond with something- anything. I have no idea why that just came out of my mouth.

"You have no idea," He tells me but he still doesn't move any closer to me like I kind of expected him to.

I'm starting to find it hard to believe that I'm going to have the will power to make it through this trip in one piece. "It won't fix anything," I say quickly under my breath. "It'll just complicate things even more."

"But you want to kiss me too," He says it as a statement, not a question, but I feel like I need to answer anyway.

I shrug and look down at my lap instead of up at Andrew. "I… I mean, yeah but it's just such a bad idea. We should talk first. Be adults and everything."

"Right. Of course."

"But I'm tired of making the smart decision," I say before I even make the decision to say it at all. Once again, my mouth is speaking without my brain's permission. "And I miss you so much so you have about three seconds before I change my mind."

"Are you sure?" He questions me softly. "I want to do this right, Stell."

I look up at him and I can feel myself leaning toward him- or maybe he's leaning toward me, I can't really tell- and then I nod. "I think so."

And then, without any more talking, he leans in, closing the rest of the distance between us. The feeling of his lips on mine makes me let out an involuntary gasp. It's been so long since I've kissed him and I've missed it more than I even realized. For a long, heart-stopping moment, our lips just stay there, pressed together and unmoving as if we're familiarizing ourselves with each other again. Remembering each other's contours, how it feels. I also think that Andrew doesn't move for a minute to wait and see if I'm going to change my mind but it's too late- I'm too far gone now.

When I don't pull away, Andrew leans closer to me and wraps his hand around in my hair before he begins moving his lips against mine. I shake out of the shock of the kiss and start to move against him as well. It's not slow by any means. We've been apart for so long that this kiss is like a breath of fresh air. It's like I've been drowning since the day that we broke up and now- this kiss- it feels like I've resurfaced. I can finally breathe.

I rotate my body so that I'm completely facing Andrew and I lean farther into him, deepening the kiss a little bit. He groans in the back of his throat and I remind myself to breathe although it's getting continuously harder to do so. I hold back an instinctive moan before I realize that it's stupid to hold back now. We're already kissing so we might as well just enjoy it before the awkwardness and drama seep back into our lives.

With this in mind, I run my fingers through his blond hair and then run my tongue along his bottom lip. This point in time is the exact moment when all hell broke loose inside of both of us. Desperate to keep breathing each other in, my fist clenches in his hair and his hand that was in my hair moves to firmly grip my shoulder, pushing me back onto the bed so that we're laying down in a mangled horizontal mess.

There's moaning and there's groaning and hair pulling and clothes being shuffled. Every nerve in my body is on edge, every skin-to-skin touch is like fire on my skin causing me to tremble in a mess of goose bumps. With my hand up his shirt, I start feverishly kissing his jawline, nipping at his skin a little bit with my teeth which I know he likes.

I can't believe this is happening. Just a little while ago, I was so angry at Andrew that I could have pushed him off of a low-rise bridge but now, we're kissing like we just got hitched or something. It's such a drastic change in our relationship and I'm not sure how we're going to deal with this after today but right now, it feels like a pretty nice change. Then maybe, this is just something that I don't need to overthink. It's just something nice that's happening and that's it. There's no thinking about it- no worrying about the next step- there's just enjoying what we have right here. Right now.

"Stella," Andrew groans my name before pressing his lips to mine again, his hand playing with the button of my jean shorts but not actually unbuttoning them.

I've missed this so much that it's almost painful to stop but I know that we have to before his mom or brother come up to get us for dinner. Or maybe his dad will arrive and want to see Andrew. No matter what, one of us has to regain some sense before we take things too far.

I leave one more lingering kiss on his lips and I think that he knows by the calmness of the kiss that this has to be the end of whatever just happened. I press my hands to his chest- outside of his shirt this time- and then he sits up. There's a sudden coldness without his body against mine but I take the separation and silence to catch my breath.

I smooth my t-shirt out again since it had shifted up my body when I was laying down and then I run my fingers through my hair. "I need to take a walk."

"Stell," Andrew starts to say as if he's about to apologize for something.

"No, it's fine," I say quickly, not wanting him to apologize for what just happened as if it was a mistake and it was all his fault. "I'm not mad or anything but I just need to clear my head for a little bit."

He nods in understanding and then I stand up off of the bed and walk out of the room to go into the bathroom. Other than my lips being red and a little swollen, I don't look conspicuous at all so I slip my shoes back on and then I walk downstairs and out the front door without encountering either Marie or Lucas.

My only goal for this vacation was to make my life less complicated. I haven't even been here for twelve hours and I've already failed.

19 Discussions

"Stella," Somebody begins to shake me awake the next morning. "You have to wake up, Stell."

"No I don't," I mumble into the pillow.

"Yes, you do," He laughs- it's Andrew and he has a hand on my shoulder. My back is a little sore from sleeping on the floor in his room but other than that, I was surprisingly comfortable. Andrew tried to let me take the bed but I'd feel too guilty if I took his bed away from him and I didn't want to sleep down on couch in fear of somebody else walking in on me sleeping. It freaks me out to know that people can see me sleep because I know that I snore sometimes and it's just ugly. Andrew's obviously seen me sleeping before though so it doesn't bother me, which is why I wanted to sleep in his room last night, just not in his bed. He gave me a pillow and an extra blanket to sleep with and with that, I was fine.

"Why?" I whine, feeling my sleepiness begin to fade a little bit so I turn around and open my eyes, seeing Andrew hovering over top of me, crouched beside me.

I hear him chuckle a little bit before responding. "Breakfast is almost ready."

"Pancakes?"

"Yes, there are pancakes," He assures me, which is a huge motivation for me to get up. His mom makes really amazing pancakes so he doesn't have to ask me again to wake up with that promise of pancakes. I sit up and run my fingers through my hair before looking up at him.

"You better not be lying," I warn him.

He chuckles again and helps me to my feet. "I'm not lying. My mom made pancakes. You have time to take a shower if you want before we go downstairs."

"Yeah, I want to do that," I nod. "Shower, pancakes, and then we need to talk. Like, a real conversation that doesn't end in either yelling or kissing."

"Okay. But would it really be terrible if we kissed a little?" He jokes with a cheeky grin.

I softly shove his shoulder. "You're such an idiot."

He just laughs as I gather an outfit from my suitcase and leave the room to go across the hallway and into the bathroom to take a quick shower before facing the day.

When I get back into Andrew's room, I'm wearing a black maxi skirt and a pink blouse. I knock on his door just in case he's getting dressed and when he calls from the other side that I can come in, I open the door and walk inside. I'm stopped cold in my tracks when I look up and see that Andrew is sitting on his bed texting somebody, which would be completely normal if he had a shirt on.

"You're an ass," I mumble under my breath as I toss my pajamas into my suitcase and then turn around so that I can't see him anymore.

"What?" He wonders in confusion. "What'd I do?"

"You just are," I huff. "Are you ready to go downstairs now?"

"Yeah, give me a sec," He says and then I hear rustling around as he stands up from the bed and, I assume, puts a shirt on. I wait patiently looking the other way because I know- and he knows too- that I turn to goop whenever he doesn't have a shirt on because his torso is just so nice to look at. However, I don't want to look at it right now because it'd be so unfair to look at it but not be allowed to touch it.

"That was definitely not nice," I mumble as we leave his room and go downstairs.

He laughs a little bit from behind me. "I still don't know what I did."

"Yes you do," I sigh but that's the end of the conversation since we enter the kitchen where Marie, Lucas, and their father, Cole, are sitting around a large dining room table.

"Good morning, sleepy heads," Marie chirps when she notices us walking into the room. I sit down in a chair beside Andrew and across from Lucas as I eagerly start to pile the pancakes onto my plate since everybody else has already began to eat which means that I need to get as many as I can now before they're all gone.

"Good morning," I say through a yawn but I'm not sure what else to say. We covered all of the basics last night at dinner- how our travel went, the winter dance show, all of the stuff that we should have shared with them was shared last night at dinner after Cole got home from work and we all went out to dinner to celebrate Andrew's coming home.

"So, Stella, what is your family doing for Christmas? I'm surprised that you didn't go home for the holidays," Cole tells as I'm politely devouring my pancakes.

"They're not doing anything," I say, making sure to swallow before answering him. "My parents have a charity thing going on in Chicago and my brother went to some ski resort with his friends. My family isn't really big on holidays."

"Well, we missed you during Thanksgiving," He tells me. "You were with your family then, right?"

I nod in confirmation. "Yeah. We have one holiday a year just to remind ourselves why we're not big on holidays. It was pretty much a disaster."

"I'm sorry to hear that, dear," Marie frowns sympathetically.

"That's okay," I shrug. "I'd much rather be here eating your amazing pancakes than in Tennessee dealing with the snow anyway."

"Well, we had already done all of our gift shopping before Andrew told us that you were coming, so I didn't even think to get you anything special for Christmas. I guess we'll just put something together last minute," Marie says with a polite smile. "It'll be fun."

"Oh. No," I say quickly. "Really, you don't have to get me anything for Christmas. I'm already kind of invading your holiday as it is."

"Nonsense," She scoffs. "We love that you're here, Stella. The more the merrier, especially during the holidays."

"Thanks," I offer her a small smile as I continue to devour my pancakes. "I really do appreciate you guys letting me spend our break here."

"Of course, dear," She chirps. "You're always welcome here."

"So, we're going to go over to the mall after breakfast," Andrew speaks up from beside me after a long time of him being oddly silent. "If that's okay, Mom?"

"Sure. Of course. As long as you bring me back some of that raspberry tea from the tea shop," Marie nods. "You know that stuff that I always get?"

"Yeah, I can pick you up some of that," He confirms. "I'm not sure how long we'll be out but we should be back before dinnertime. We might go see a movie too."

"Busy day?" Lucas wonders with a small laugh.

I blush and look down at my plate, continuing to eat and to try and pretend like I didn't catch his double meaning.

"Not that busy, Luke," Andrew rolls his eyes at his brother. "Just going around town and everything."

"Be safe," Cole warns us as I'm finishing up my pancakes and then I notice Andrew stand up from his chair, so I do the same.

"Yeah, we'll be fine. See you guys later," Andrew says before leading me towards the front door of the house. Marie calls a goodbye but before I can respond, we're already out the door and headed for Andrew's car.

"I didn't know that we were going to the mall," I tell him but I still get into the passenger side of his car because I don't really have a problem with going to the mall or anything, I just didn't know that he had it planned or something.

"I think it's a good place for us to talk," He explains.

"Where there's witnesses," I say jokingly.

Andrew laughs a little bit and then nods. "Exactly."

There's a small silence and then I look out the window, resting my elbow on the car door and my chin rests on my knuckles. "I missed your mom. She's really amazing, you know."

"Yeah. I know," He nods. "And you're like, her favorite person ever."

"Yeah?" I wonder with raised eyebrows. "What makes me so special?"

Andrew shrugs. "I mean, you are pretty amazing. I think she knows how happy that you make me and that just makes her love you. It's that simple with her- if it makes me happy, it makes her happy. The same thing with Luke, really. She's really selfless."

"Most mothers are," I mumble, leaving an awkward silence in the air afterwards, which I didn't intend to happen but now, we're both thinking the same thing- my mother isn't one of those 'most moms' that's selfless like that. She doesn't drop everything for her kids- not even once has she ever done that- and my happiness is not the equivalent to hers. She loves me a lot, I know that she does, but she's just such a cold person that she has no idea how to express it.

"Well, like I told them, we can go see a movie. The theater is in the mall and I'm sure something is playing that you want to see," Andrew finally speaks after a few minutes of silence as we're driving down the road.

"I guess it'll depend on how well this first part goes and then we'll see," I suggest. "I still can't tell if this is a really good idea or a really bad one."

"I'm putting my money on the really good one," He offers with a slightly forced smile.

"I'm hoping," I say. "But I know that there's still a lot that can go wrong. I don't want to fight anymore but it's going to be difficult considering everything that's happened."

"I know," He sighs. "Hey, but let's save the serious talk for the mall where we can sit and really talk, alright? We don't have to think about it right now. We can go walk around the mall for a little while. Just enjoy each other's company before we talk about the serious stuff."

"Are you going to buy me those cinnamon pretzel stick things?" I wonder with a playful smile, trying to keep the mood light. Andrew's plan seems like a wonderful idea- to just enjoy each other's company for a little while and then start talking about the heavy stuff. I miss him more than I'll ever be willing to admit, so just being with him, ignoring all of the problems that we have, it all seems wonderful right now.

"Sure, Stell," He chuckles. "But you have to share them with me."

"I guess that's fair," I sigh. "We'll have to wait though, since we just had breakfast. I'm holding you to this, though. You know how I get when there's free food on the table."

"Yeah," He laughs again. "I know."

"Does this mall have a shoe store?" I wonder. "I wouldn't mind a little bit of shoe shopping."

"No," Andrew says quickly. "This mall is strictly shoe store-less."

"Why do I have a feeling that you're lying?" I ask him with raised eyebrows.

He shrugs, pulling into the busy parking lot of the large mall. "I have no idea. I assure you though, there really are no shoes to be purchased at this mall. It's some kind of shoe ban or something."

I can't help but laugh at his obvious lie and I roll my eyes. I know that I do get a little intense while going shoe shopping and Andrew's experienced that first hand when I drag him along with me to the mall in LA, which is probably why he's joking around right now, because he doesn't want to go shoe shopping with me right now. "Yeah. I'm sure that's it. Fine. We won't go shoe shopping. What other kind of stores are there? Clothes?"

"Nope," He shakes his head. He finds a parking spot close to the entrance upon some lovely miracle and then we both get out of the car to walk inside. "I think here's some video game stores, there's CDs and food. They're against shoes and clothes though. It's weird."

"Funny," I say. "You are to video games as I am to shoes, you know."

"I am not that bad, Stell," He scoffs as if that's so ridiculous when in reality, I'm being completely honest.

"You are just as bad as me," I insist. "It takes you hours to pick out a video game or anything that has to do with electronics."

"Electronics are way more expensive than clothes and shoes," He counters in justification.

"Yeah right," I scoff jokingly. "My favorite pair of heels cost more than your beloved Xbox so that argument is completely invalid."

"Seriously?" He wonders incredulously. "You spent that much on just one pair of shoes?"

I shrug innocently as we walk through the front entrance into the mall and I start to look around, looking at all of the different types of stores around us, noticing a large fountain in the center of everything where there's a small girl tossing a coin into the water. "They make my butt look good."

"Your butt always looks good," Andrew tells me. "You don't need expensive shoes to do that for you."

I blush and look away from him. "No flirting. Anyway, they're really cute and it's my parents' money. They barely even notice my credit card bills. And remember the red lingerie that I wore on your birthday? That took me hours to pick out so you really shouldn't complain about me taking too long to shop."

"That wasn't flirting?"

I shake my head. "No, I'm just defending my shopping tactics and proving you wrong, which is what I do best."

"Adorable," He chuckles teasingly. "I guess we have to agree to disagree. No clothes or video games."

"Well, what does that leave us?" I ask him. "Movies and food?"

"There's a Sears, Hot Topic, and a FYE. Those are the three that come to mind," He informs me. "Or we can just walk around and talk."

"Window shopping is my best talent," I say with a small smile.

He scoffs and rolls his eyes at me. "Yeah, I'm sure that's your best talent."

I drop my jaw at his perverted insinuation and when he sees me giving him that look, Andrew only laughs and continues walking down the wide tiled aisle of the mall.

"Jeez, Stell. Get your head out of the gutter, okay? I was talking about your dancing."

I blush again- something that only Andrew can make me do and it's incredibly unfair- and look away from him, awkwardly clearing my throat. "Yeah. I knew that. What did you think that I thought you meant?"

And then, Andrew does this adorable thing where he tries not to smile but he still smiles, not able to hold it back, and then it sprouts into a full out grin. "We both know what you were thinking. I do believe that you just made it clear that we weren't allowed to flirt though, and I feel like talking about the type of thing that you're thinking about deliberately breaks that rule."

"This is impossible," I mutter with a small laugh.

As we walk around the mall, we seem to be doing a fantastic job at avoiding the big awkward cloud hovering over our heads. Why we're really here, what has to happen after our lengthy walk around the mall, just enjoying each other's company. I don't want to sit down and talk about the serious stuff because I like what we have right now. I like just walking around with Andrew and hanging out with him and laughing with him as if nothing is wrong at all. It's the happiest I've felt in an incredibly long time and I don't want to let go of it.

However, once we've walked around the upper level and then use the escalator to move down to the first floor, we walk through the aisle until we get to the food court and I know that it's time for us to pop our optimistic bubble and get down to business.

"So we can get those pretzels now," Andrew clears his throat when he seems my face fall a little bit when we approach the food court.

I nod and then start walking towards the pretzel kiosk, waiting for Andrew to follow me there.

"Is there something wrong?" He wonders as we stand in line with just a few people in front of us at the counter.

"No, I'm fine," I assure him but I know that by the way that I'm staring down at my shoes and how I'm playing with the sides of my skirt that he can tell that I'm lying.

"Stella, we're just going to talk," He reminds me, nudging my shoulder with his own which is a way that he subtly likes to comfort me without being too overbearing. Just a little nudge of the shoulder to let me know that he's still there. "It's going to be fine."

"Right. I know," I assure him even though I'm still not so sure.

He nudges my shoulder again and this time, I nudge back. We fall silent until we order our pretzels and then find a small table near wall so that we're not near all of the foot traffic. It's as close to privacy as we can get on a busy area in the mall.

"I love these pretzels," I say, trying to make the mood light again but I know that it's a lost cause.

"Stella," He says my name quietly, watching me with a slightly uneasy look.

"Yeah. I know, we need to talk. That's why we're here," I mumble after eating only one of my pretzel sticks.

"Stell, you don't have to be so nervous," He assures me again. "This is going to be good for us."

"I don't even know what else there is to talk about. We've pretty much covered all of the important stuff," I say but then I think of something and I pause to try and decide if I should say it or not. I need to think before I speak so that I don't say anything that I might regret.

"What is it? You can say whatever you want to say," Andrew tells me with an assuring nod as he looks at me, waiting for me to say what I want to say.

I take a deep breath as I'm looking up at the ceiling. "I'm trying- and I'm going to continue to try- to work things out with you. I do want to work things out with you, Andrew. I just want you to know that it isn't mandatory for me to do so. I don't have to forgive you. I can live without you. Even if I don't want to, I can do it. You do not own me. I do love you so much but I am my own person and it is possible for me to move on, no matter how painful."

He nods and leans forward. "I know that, Stell. You're one of the strongest people that I know."

"I just wanted that to be clear," I mumble softly, nibbling on the end of another soft pretzel stick. "Other than that though, I don't know what else there is to say."

"Well, I've already said that I'm sorry," He tells me. "I'm not so sure that I know what we should talk about either but I know that we need to talk about something."

"What do you want to happen after today?" I ask him curiously, continuing to slowly nibble on my soft pretzel.

"I want to take you out," He responds without any hesitation. "On a… second first date."

I sigh and shake my head a little bit. "Dinner and a movie won't fix this."

He laughs a little and leans forward with his elbows on the table. "I'm disappointed that you think that I'd expect you to settle for dinner and a movie."

"You did the first time," I remind him.

"Yeah, but it was romantically cute the first time," He justifies. "This time, I'm really going to blow your mind."

"I never said yes," I say quietly. "I'm still not sure if I'm ready to go back on a date or something."

"Okay, well then I think that it's your turn to answer the question. What do you want to happen after today?" He fires my question back at me.

I'm not surprised that he's asking me this but what catches me by surprise is that I have no idea how to answer that. What do I want from this? I'm not ready to agree to go on a date but I'm also not really angry at him anymore. I don't want to get back in a relationship yet but the only reason that I came with him to New Mexico was so that we could rekindle our relationship.

Everything inside of me is contradictory and I have no idea how to think or how to respond to his question.

"I..." I trail off as I force myself to think up an answer. A true answer. "I do think that we'll get back together. That's what I want. And you know that I love you. I really do. It's just that you... you really hurt me so much. I was giving you everything I had but you were treating me like I was just somebody that you had to deal with. For my whole life, I've just been somebody to deal with and it took me a very long time to get myself to believe that I was more than that. That I deserve more than that. You were ruining that though and I felt like complete shit all of the time. I deserve more than that."

"I know that you do," He assures me. "And I never meant to make you feel like that. I got a lot carried away with everything and I didn't realize how much it affected you and I'm sorry. It'll never happen again. You know that, right?"

"How could I possibly know that?" I ask him. "I never thought that it would happen before it happened but you still did it."

"But now that I realize what it did to you, I've learned my lesson. I'll never treat you like that again, Stell," He assures me. "You know that saying, 'you don't know what you have until it's gone' or something like that? I didn't realize how much I'm incredibly in love with you until you broke up with me. It hurt like hell to see you like that. I'll treat you like the freaking Queen of Sheba just give me another chance. Please, Stella."

I look down at the table, swallow hard, and then look up at Andrew. "We have two weeks. I want us to be okay but I also want to take it slow. To make sure that this is really what I want and that it's really what you want. There is nothing that I want more than to be as happy as we used to be but we just have to take it slow."

"Okay..." He trails off, seemingly confused as to what I'm suggesting. "So where does that leave us?"

"It means that you have two weeks to remind me why I ever fell in love with you. We have two weeks to start from the beginning and just... I don't know, start over. If we're meant to be then it'll work out. Two weeks is a long time, you know? It'll work."

He looks at me intently and I bite my lip, waiting anxiously for his response. He makes it seem like I'm the one calling the shots but I know that he won't wait forever. I'm afraid that by making this decision, it might be his breaking point. Anything could be his breaking point, where he decides that enough is enough and just walks away. When he realizes that I'm not worth all of the waiting and working it out.

"Okay," He nods and I let out a breath that I'd been holding. "I can convince you in two weeks."

A smile twitches at the corner of my mouth. "I hope that you do," I say quietly, taking another bite of my pretzel.

"There is one problem though," Andrew says, reaching his hand over the table to grab mine in his. I almost pull away because we shouldn't hold hands- especially not right now- but instead, I find myself holding on to him, gripping his hand tightly.

"What is it?" I ask him, frowning in confusion.

He tries to hide his grin, which is –like I've said before- the cutest thing that I have ever seen, and holds my hand tighter. "It's going to really suck having to wait two more weeks to kiss you again."

Blushing, I look away from him. "Andrew."

"Sorry, I know. No flirting. That was it though. Okay well, probably not but I'll try. A little," He assures me.

I finish my last pretzel stick and playfully roll my eyes at him. "We should probably get back to your house. We've been gone for a while."

"Sure. But what do you want me to tell my mom? I mean you said that you want me to tell her that we're not together, which is totally fine, but if there's a chance that we're going to get back together soon then it'll just confuse her."

"She's your mom," I say as if he doesn't already know that. "You can decide what you want to tell her."

"You're amazing," He tells me. "I mean, I know that you already know that I know how amazing you are but I just feel like I should tell you anyway."

"I'll never get tired of hearing you say that," I assure him.

"You're really sending me mixed signals with this 'no flirting' rule, you know," He teases me as we both stand up from the table and start to leave the mall.

Again, I playfully roll my eyes at him and nudge him with my shoulder. "I change my mind."

He grins at me and my heart speeds up a little bit like a lovesick puppy. "That's extremely good to hear."

I laugh and then glance up at him, hoping that this will work. That we will get our second chance and maybe- hopefully- we'll get it right this time.

20 Shopping

"I think that this is a brilliant idea," Mason tells me over the phone. "You and Andrew desperately need to get it together."

"I know," I sigh. "I think we're doing okay."

"So you're not fighting anymore? Why do I find that hard to believe?" She wonders skeptically.

"You know, there was a time that we made a really adorable couple," I remind her as I sit down on the edge of Andrew's bed and start running my fingers through my wet blonde hair. I'd just taken a shower since Andrew and his whole family went to visit Marie's parents a few hours away. It's Christmas Eve and tomorrow, there's a huge Christmas party at Andrew's uncle's house but because Marie's mother can't do road trips, they drove up there to celebrate Christmas on Christmas Eve with her parents. They invited me to go with them but I declined since I thought that it'd be awkward to join in on their small family gathering when I've never even met Marie's parents. "We're working things out."

"Well, good for you. I'm happy for you guys," She says. "Just please don't get pregnant while you're gone. You have a bright future."

I let out a little laugh. "Did you join a teen pregnancy prevention club while I've been gone?"

"Okay, excuse me for not wanting one of my best friends to wreck her future with a baby. I mean, right now is when you're the most vulnerable. You're excited and happy to be back together and all reasonable thinking just goes out the door," She tells me slightly joking.

"I never said that we were back together," I tell her.

"I know but that's just because you like to complicate things," She says and I can practically hear her eyes roll through the phone. "Once you are back together, though, make sure that you take precautions."

"It's not complicated, Mase," I laugh at her. "We're just taking it slow. And again, I'm not going to get pregnant. We're at his parents' house for God's sake."

"Yeah, you should probably wait until you get back then," Mason agrees with me. "Anyway though, I'm still excited that you guys aren't fighting anymore."

"I think everybody's excited for this," I mutter with a small laugh. "I think he's planning something big. Probably for after the Christmas party or New Year's but he's being suspicious about something."

"He is somebody who'd do something romantic like that," She says. "But I didn't know that you were going to a Christmas party. With his family?"

"Yeah, it's a big party at his uncle's house or something. It'll probably be majorly awkward considering I don't really know any of his family except for his parents and his brother. I don't even know how he's going to introduce me to his family considering his parents still think that we're really together. Big families always make me a little nervous," I explain to her as I grab the remote to his TV and turn it on, turning it to a station that I like to watch.

"See? I told you that it's complicated," She chuckles. "But you'll do fine. Just go with it and relax. His family is really nice. I mean, I've only met his parents but I'm just assuming that they're all as nice as his parents, so you don't have anything to worry about."

"I hope they're all as nice as his parents," I sigh. "Andrew says that they're nice but he could just be saying that to make me feel better about it. It didn't work very well though. I'm not nervous that much about meeting his family as much as I am about seeing his family and comparing it to mine. His family is like, everything that mine isn't and it's really awesome that he has all of these amazing people around him, you know? It just sucks that whenever I'm with his parents, I'm wishing that mine could be more like them. It just sucks."

"Does Andrew know that?" She wonders quietly.

"No. It's not a big deal, really, it's just a thing," I assure her. "I don't want him to feel bad or anything. He shouldn't feel bad but I know that he would if I told him something like that."

"You're too kind," Mason jokes. "Seriously, though, you should open up to him with that kind of stuff. Isn't that what you guys are doing now? Opening up and everything?"

"Yeah, yeah," I sigh. "We're still figuring things out. It'll be fine."

"Okay then... if you say so," She sings through the phone.

"Well, how's your vacation going so far?" I ask her to change the subject from me and onto Mason.

"I've been living like a potato," She tells me. "I'm either eating, sleeping, or hanging out with Brian and/or Sienna. It's basically paradise and I might just never go back to school."

"Yeah," I scoff. "Just a few more months and then you won't have to go back."

"Right. This vacation is just nice, I guess. Tomorrow will probably be my busiest day since Brian is coming to my family's Christmas party and then we're going over to his family's Christmas dinner which means that we'll only have tomorrow night to celebrate our own private Christmas."

"Don't go into details please," I joke with a small laugh.

"No, I don't mean it like that, you pervert," She chuckles. "I just mean that a few hours by ourselves will be nice on the holiday. And you remember what I got for him? I can't wait to see his face when he opens it."

"Yeah, he's going to love it. Anyway, I should go get something for Andrew before they get back," I decide. "He probably got something for me and I'd feel shitty if I don't get him something too."

"Gift shipping is so hard for guys. I mean, us girls are so easy because just a cute little necklace or a romantically personal bracelet is all we need to break out into tears but guys... it took me forever to find the perfect thing."

"Yeah. Well, I have about two and a half hours to find the perfect thing so I guess I'll need a miracle. I have no idea what I could get him that's not too romantic and personal but still a great gift," I explain to her.

"You need to stop talking to me then," Mason jokes. "You need to get thinking like, yesterday."

"I know. You're right," I agree with her. I hadn't decided if I should get Andrew a present yet because I wasn't sure if that would be too weird or not but just now, talking to Mason, I realized that he's definitely going to get me something. That's just how he is. Even if we were still fighting, he'd make sure to get me a Christmas present. So the obvious answer is yes, I do need to get him a present. Not just because he's getting me one but because a present is a little reminder that somebody cares about you. And I do care about Andrew therefor, I need to get him a present and it needs to be an awesome one. "Well, I should go figure this out. I'll talk to you later?"

"Yeah, we'll talk later. I want to know how this goes so call me later," She tells me.

"Right," I chuckle. "I'll do that. Merry Christmas, Mase."

"Merry Christmas, Stell," She chimes before hanging up.

I toss my phone into my large purse and then grab Andrew's keys from his nightstand. He rode with his parents in their car to their relatives and Andrew said that if I want to go anywhere that I can use his car. He made a joking remark about making sure that I don't get lost and then he gave me the keys.

I have no idea where to go or how to get there considering I've only been to New Mexico one time before and we spent all of that time here at Andrew's house. Before I get to leave the house, I pull out my laptop and start to search for stores nearby that sell types of things that I can get for Andrew for Christmas. The issue with this, however, is that I have no idea what to get him that lies between friendship and relationship.

It takes me a little while to get a small list of addresses to stores that might have something that I can get for him. Most of the stores are expensive versions of Sears which might not be the best idea but I'm hoping that it'll jog some ideas free in my brain.

I scribble down the addresses and leave a note for Andrew that I'm going shopping just in case they get back before I do and then I get in the car and head off to the closest store. Just a few steps inside, I get a whiff of pure masculinity and overcompensation. There's an electronics area with TVs and laptops and then there's a clothes section that looks a lot simpler than the clothes sections that I'm used to considering this store is strictly for men so there's no purple (real men might wear pink but purple is just out of the question) or frills or skirts or anything exciting. And then there's tools and watches and ties and cologne that's filling the whole entire store with a potent stench.

As I'm walking through the aisles of all of the belts and appliances, I notice a few middle-aged men giving me strange looks as they inspect their high end DVD players and suit jackets. I suspect it's because I'm a bit misplaced in this store that basically sells masculinity when, in contrast, I am basically the definition of femininity. This store and I are like mortal enemies. I push through it though because I hope that if I can't find a gift here, I can at least get an idea.

I pass by a few other people- there are some men who are probably searching for those Christmas sales and then there are some women who are most likely hastily grabbing some last minute Christmas gift, much like myself. I doubt that these women have such complicated relationships with their gift receivers.

I can't buy him something ridiculous like a tie. A tie is something that you give your father or grandpa. He already has a nice TV in his dorm so I can't get him a TV either.

"Hello. Can I help you with anything?" I hear somebody ask me as they approach me while I'm looking at a shelf of iPads even though I'm pretty sure that I'm not going to get him one.

"Um, no thanks," I say politely. "Just some last minute gift shopping."

"Having trouble?" He wonders jokingly.

"Tons," I sigh.

"Well, I know I probably shouldn't say this because it's bad for business but you're not going to find an awesome gift here."

"No?"

The guy, who looks to be in his twenties with a polo with the store's logo on the front, nods at me and leans against the shelf. "I mean, stuff that you buy here is so generic- for people who don't have time to think of anything else. But you're young, you should go creative."

"I have like, eighteen hours," I remind him, realizing how close we are to Christmas day by looking down at my phone. "I don't have time to be creative."

He shrugs. "You just have to work harder for it."

I bite my lip, thinking about what he just said. Make it personal. Show Andrew that I really know him. One thing immediately comes to mind and I know that, although it sounds impossible, it sounds like it could be the best gift ever- one that isn't too romantic or too platonic. It's perfect. "Yeah. Okay, that gives me an idea. Thanks."

"No problem," He sings before walking away, swinging his lanyard of keys around his finger. "Good luck."

I hurry out of the electronics section and towards the small area where they have their pretentious collection of coffees and teas and then stare at all of the displays for a long time to attempt to decide which one to buy because I can't remember what kind of coffee that he likes, I just remember that it's fancy. I try to remember but I just can't do it so I finally just decide to grab the most expensive type of coffee they have that fit my plan and then head for the front of the store to check out.

It's almost my turn in line to check out when I hear my phone start ringing in my pocket. I jump a little before hurrying to grab it and answer, checking the caller ID first to see that it's Andrew.

"Hey," I chirp into the phone.

"Hey, are you still out shopping? I got your note," He tells me.

"Yeah, I should be done soon. You're back early," I note, realizing that they were only gone for six hours which means that they only got to spend about two hours actually there considering the long drive. "I thought you'd be gone for at least a few more hours."

"It was kind of an awkward visit," He informs me dismissively. "What on earth could you be shopping for on Christmas Eve?"

"Just some stuff," I say vaguely. "I got hungry and decided to go find food."

"Okay then…" He chuckles slowly as I'm giving my money to the cashier. "Well, I'll see you soon then."

"Yeah, I'm on my way back now," I tell him before we say goodbye and then hang up so that I can drive back to his house.

Luckily, when I came into the house, Andrew was in his room so I was able to hide his present in the hall closet behind some towels before he realized that I'd gotten there. When I get to the house, everybody else is gone. Andrew tells me that his parents went to his uncle's house to help set up for the big party tomorrow and Lucas went out somewhere but Andrew isn't entirely sure where exactly his brother is.

"So, what are we going to do with the rest of the day?" I ask Andrew as we're walking up into his room.

"Well, I know what I want to do but I wouldn't really consider them platonic and you know, you have your rules and everything," He explains teasingly. "So what do you want to do?"

I roll my eyes at him and silently wish that he'd stop being so teasing but I don't actually ask him to stop because he'd just tease me even more. "I don't know. Do you have board games? Because I can totally kick your ass at whatever games you have."

He laughs and shrugs. "I might have something in the back of my closet maybe. But whatever it is, I promise you that you won't beat me at it."

I sit down on the edge of his bed and watch as he opens his closet and then he steps on his tippy toes to reach the top shelf of his closet and he reaches back and then pulls out a square box. "Checkers?" I read the front of the box with raised eyebrows. "The only game you have is checkers?"

"Were you expecting a huge collection of board games in my closet?" He laughs a little bit, tossing the game onto the bed beside me.

"I was hoping," I tease him, opening the box and then taking out the board and the small circular chip-like pawns. "The only way that checkers is just a little amusing is if it's strip checkers." Ha, Andrew! You're not the only one that can tease.

"That is a wonderful idea," Andrew grins at me. "Especially since I can really kick your ass and you'd end up naked."

I scoff as we start to lay out the red and black pieces. "You wish. We're not doing that, though."

He shrugs and the shine in his eyes almost takes my breath away. "Can't blame me for trying."

21 Christmas Time

"I am so exhausted," Marie says as she plops down on the couch with her eyes drooping open and closed. "So much holiday spirit in one day is a lot to take."

We just got back from the Haggerty Christmas party and Marie is right- it was pretty exhausting to meet his whole family and be introduced to everybody at the party. I don't remember any of the names at all but Andrew introduced me to almost everybody. Aunts, uncles, cousins, second cousins, they were all there. I'm sure barely any of them remembered my name and I was mostly just referred to as 'Andrew's friend' which was fine with me because I wouldn't remember anybody's names either. I was stuffed too because of all of the food that was there. Apparently, it's a requirement in the family that you have to be an incredible chef and then you must cook something incredible for the Christmas party. Most of the time, I watch what I eat but this Christmas party broke me.

"I didn't know that Aunt Jen got married," Lucas says randomly, hanging his jacket up on the coat rack before heading upstairs, obviously pretty tired from the party as well.

"She eloped last year," Marie reminds him.

"Yeah, well we're going to go upstairs now so we'll see you guys in the morning," Andrew says before wrapping his arm around my shoulders and leading me towards the stairs behind Lucas.

When we get into his room, he shuts the door and then we're alone to celebrate our own personal little Christmas.

"So, do I get my present now?" I ask him jokingly, sitting on the edge of his bed.

He nods and teasingly rolls his eyes at me. "Yeah, it's in here," He says, going into the closet and grabbing a wrapped box. "Do I get my present too?"

"Not yet," I smile up at him as he hands me the box. "But it's a really good present so it'll be worth the wait, I think."

"Okay then," He chuckles. "Go ahead and open yours then and prepare to be amazed."

"I better be amazed," I joke.

"Just open it," He rolls his eyes at me.

I tug on the paper until it rips and look at the box but it's a completely unexciting plain brown box. I tear open the tape and look in the box, moving around some tissue paper to find a small black box that looks like it holds jewelry. It's long so it's either a bracelet or maybe a necklace.

"I know that it may be too romantic," Andrew explains. "And incredibly cliché, but I bought it before everything happened and I was still going to give it to you no matter what because I really think that you'd like it."

I eagerly grab the black box and push it open to see a beautiful golden bracelet inside made up of connected music notes with diamonds on some of the round part of the notes. "Wow," I breathe, pulling it out of the box and holding it in my fingers to feel the smooth gold.

"Flip it over," He tells me. "I know that you have all of the money in the world so if you wanted a bracelet then you could just buy one, which is why I had to make it special- something that you can't just buy."

I look at the back of the music notes and I can tell that there's letters engraved in the back of the notes that read "AWH 7-24-13" with one character on each note. AWH being his initials and July 24th being the date that we got together over the summer. "This is amazing, Andrew," I tell him with a small smile. "Really, I love it."

"Good," He takes the bracelet from me, silently offering to clasp it around my wrist for me and when he does, I inspect it again- it really is an amazing and personal gift and it's so perfect that I just want to lean forward and kiss him but I know that I can't do that. We're still just friends and, although I'm sure that that will end soon, I have to stick with it for now. I compromise with myself by leaning forward and kissing his cheek, which is a friendly gesture.

"Your present is downstairs, so I'll be right back," I tell him, standing up off of the bed to go downstairs. While I'm down there, I send a picture of the bracelet to Mason and Sienna because I'm just that excited about it and then I wish them a Merry Christmas as I'm gathering up Andrew's present.

I go back into his room with two coffee mugs full of that expensive coffee mixed with cream and sugar and I hand one of them to Andrew.

"A cup of coffee?" He wonders with amusement.

I nod. "Yep. Drink it though, it's really good coffee."

"Okay then," He chuckles, taking a sip of the hot coffee. "Wow, it is really good. This is almost as awesome as a Christmas miracle."

"Shut up," I softly nudge him. "It's Swiss coffee. That's why it tastes so good."

"I feel like you're leading up to something," He eyes me suspiciously.

I nod, pulling a small box out of my bag that's been sitting on the other side of the bed. "You would be correct," I tell him, handing him the box with a cute little bow on the top but it isn't actually wrapped, it's just a brown square, similar to a jewelry box.

He opens it up to look at the watch that is glistening inside of the box. "Wow. This is a really nice watch," He observes, taking it out of the box to inspect it.

"It's not engraved but I can totally get it engraved if you want," I tell him quickly. "Anyway, this is a Swiss watch, which means that it's a really awesome watch."

"Swiss coffee and a Swiss watch?" He wonders with raised eyebrows. "That's very fancy."

"I'm still leading up to something," I inform him, pulling an envelope out of my bag but I wait to give it to him so that I can explain. "I remember that you said that you've never been to Europe and that you've always wanted to see the Alps."

"Stella," Andrew deadpans. "Please tell me that you did not buy me a trip to Switzerland."

"No, of course I didn't do that," I say, handing him the envelope and as he opens it, I explain what's inside. "I bought you a trip to Italy and then a train ride into Switzerland through the Alps. I only got the idea a few days ago though, so I haven't really planned it in depth yet though."

He pulls out the paper inside of the envelope, which is just a piece of paper that I cut into a small rectangle and I drew on it to make it look like a plane ticket. It's obviously fake but I haven't had time to organize dates or anything because that can take weeks or months so there's a lot to think about but the general idea is there and it's perfect.

"No, that's too much," Andrew says, shaking his head at me. "I can't accept something so insanely expensive."

"Well, this isn't a completely selfless gift," I admit. "Of course, you have to take me with you. And you have to accept it. I already bought the plane tickets," I joke, motioning towards the pen-made plane ticket that he's holding in his hand.

"Is this the whole gift or is this just another thing leading up to the fact that you actually kidnapped the Swiss king for me to keep?" He jokes, taking another sip of his coffee.

I giggle and run my fingers over my new bracelet. "Switzerland doesn't have a king, Andrew."

"Okay, fine. This is seriously incredible, Stella," He tells me, wrapping his arms around me for a tight hug. I hug him back, letting it linger for longer than it should but it's not like hugging is a crime against friendship. And considering all of the things that we could be doing right now, hugging is by far the most innocent of them all. "I can't believe we're really going to Europe."

"Well, you should believe it because it's happening," I smile at him. "There's also one more part to your present but you can't have that one yet."

"Why not?" He wonders with a confused frown.

I offer him a mischievous smile. "It's not exactly... friendly," I tell him.

He remains confused for a moment before finally understanding what I mean and then his jaw drops for a moment before he recovers and clears his throat. "Oh. You're really killing me here, Stella."

"I know," I admit with a guilty shrug. "But I have a feeling that you have something planned for New Year's Eve. Am I right or am I right?"

"New Year's Eve?" He wonders. "I might have something in mind for that particular day maybe."

"That's what I thought," I giggle, still flying high on this holiday cheer which makes it pretty impossible for me to stop laughing. "So, I suspect that after New Year's, everything will be different. Just five more days."

"It feels like forever from now," Andrew whines, putting the watch and the fake plane ticket on the night stand along with all of the boxes and gift wrap that we've gone through tonight.

"Considering everything that we've been through, a few days shouldn't be anything," I assure him. "Taking things slow will be better for us in the end. I promise."

"Yeah, I guess it helps to look at it like that," He agrees with a nod, drinking the last of his coffee. "We should get some more of this coffee when we go to Switzerland."

I laugh and jokingly roll my eyes at him. We've had a long day and I think that it's time for bed now so I grab my pajamas out of my bag so that I can get dressed. "That definitely needs to happen, I agree. And we need to buy out their chocolate supply as well. They have the best chocolate. Now, you have to look away so that I can get dressed."

"Killing. Me," He states again but I think that he's joking. Maybe.

"Just turn around," I tell him with a small smirk fighting its way onto my face.

He reluctantly hides his face under the covers and I quickly change out of my jeans and sweater for my pajama shorts and a tank top before I give him the all clear. "Well, your present makes mine look kind of crappy and that's really unfair, you know."

"Are you kidding?" I ask him incredulously, crawling onto the bed beside Andrew and fixing my hair so that it's out of my face.

"No, I'm not," He shakes his head at me. "I got you a bracelet and you gave me a watch so they even out but then you also got me a freaking trip to Europe- the ideal trip to Europe, actually. I am never going to be able to beat that ever, you know."

"You already have," I tell him honestly. "Andrew, you gave me a Christmas. That's not something that has a comparison or any kind of real value. I've never been able to do this whole Christmas thing with a real family and with real presents but you gave me that. I honestly couldn't be happier with the way that this Christmas turned out and it's all thanks to you. Seriously, you're more incredible than you give yourself credit for."

"Even after all that I've put you through, you still think that I'm incredible?" He wonders with raised eyebrows.

I hide myself under the covers and rest my head on his shoulder. "People make mistakes. Granted, yours was pretty irritating but at least you didn't cheat on me. If you did that then there wouldn't be anything incredible about you but I know that you didn't. And it's not like I ever stopped loving you, even through everything. This is our second chance. Not forgetting everything that's happened but putting it behind us and moving on. So yeah, even after all of the shit that we've put ourselves through, I do think that you're incredible because even though you're the guy that unintentionally flirted with the she devil, you're still the guy that brings me to his family's Christmas because I don't have one of my own. And that's pretty incredible."

He gets under the covers too and wraps his arms around my shoulders. "I have no idea what I would do without you, Stella Wayne."

I smile and lean into him more. "You'd obviously crash and burn."

"Obviously," He agrees jokingly. "Merry Christmas, Stell."

I kiss his cheek again before turning off the lamp beside the bed and laying down with my pillow on one of the pillows. "Merry Christmas, Andrew."

Pleeeeaaaaasseeeee comment and VOTE! Thanks! Love you so much!

22 New Year

"Stella, we have to go," Andrew says, knocking on the bathroom door.

"Yeah, yeah," I mumble, swinging all of my hair over my left shoulder and opening the door barricading Andrew from me. "I'm ready now, we can go."

He takes a step away from the door so that I can get out and then he lets his eyes roam over my outfit- a black and gold sequin dress with three quarter sleeves and black stilettos with gold chains hanging from the backs of the shoes. I take this moment to do the same to him, to appreciate his fancy outfit too. He's wearing a suit with a light blue button up shirt but no tie.

"You look gorgeous," He tells me with a sideways smile.

My dark red lips part in a nervous smile and I blush a little bit. It's been a while since he's made me blush but tonight, he does it again. I can tell that tonight is going to change everything for us- I can just tell. Which is why I spent so much time in the bathroom fixing my makeup so that it's perfect and making sure that my nails were painted black to match my dress. I'm considering this our second first date since our first date didn't go as planned, Andrew is getting his second chance. We are both getting our second chance tonight and this time, we're going to make it right.

"Thanks," I finally breathe, following him down the hallway and then down the stairs. "You look nice too, Andrew."

"Well, I have to at least try to keep up with you," He jokes. "Now, we have to go now before my parents get back from their dinner party because my mom won't let us leave without taking an hour's worth of pictures."

"Okay," I giggle. "Let's go then. Speaking of leaving... where is it that we're going?"

Andrew chuckles as he opens the front door for me and I walk out into the darkness outside since it's already pretty late but since it's New Year's Eve, we're going to be out until at least midnight, I assume, so it makes sense that we waited until late to leave. "You know that I'm not going to tell you that."

"I know, but I might as well try anyway," I sigh with a small laugh. "It has to be really nice considering we're all dressed up though."

He nods in agreement while opening the passenger side door for me. "Yeah, it's pretty fancy. That's all I'm giving you though."

"Okay, well that's good enough for now, I guess," I sigh, getting into the car and watching as he walks around the car and into the driver seat. "I'm not sure how you can beat dinner and a movie though."

He chuckles and starts the car, backing out of the driveway. "This one isn't nearly as cheesy, but I think I may have outdid myself this time. I don't know, I guess that we'll see."

We drive for a while but because I don't know my way around this city, I can't decipher where we're going based on the direction that we're going like I usually can when we're in LA. I just watch the buildings go by and listen to the radio, neither one of us speaking.

"So things will be interesting when we get back to school on Monday," Andrew finally breaks the silence.

I groan, realizing that today is Friday and we're going back to California on Sunday, so our break is pretty much over now and there's a big mess waiting for us back at school. "It's going to suck. I mean, I love the dancing but the academics and the drama is just so gross. And then we're going to have a lot of explaining to do when we tell people that we're back together."

We're at a red light and Andrew whips his head in my direction so fast that I worry that he may have snapped his own neck or something. I don't even know if that's possible, but it was a really fast reflex. "We're going to be back together?"

I shrug and lean back in my seat. "Depending on how tonight goes. But I have faith in you," I tell him with a small giggle. "Or just to get Mason off of my back."

"She is persistent," He agrees with a nod.

"She is," I chuckle. "And there will be a lot of questions to answer, but I don't know, I think that we can make it work."

"You're so remarkable, Stella," Andrew tells me as the light turns green again and he looks back to the road to continue driving, which is fortunate because I don't want him to see my blush. "Seriously, you're just so amazing that it amazes other people how amazing you are."

"You sound ridiculous," I tell him quietly.

"Maybe," He shrugs. "But it's true."

We fall into another comfortable silence for a few more minutes before we arrive at a large building with a fancy entrance, but I don't see the name of the restaurant (I assume it's a restaurant) anywhere on the building or anything, I just see a blue carpet leading up to the fancy door and a bouncer in front of the two black glass doors.

"It looks like a strip club," I tell Andrew with a small, excited laugh. I'm not excited because I think that it's a strip club, though, I'm excited because I know that it really isn't a strip club and I'm excited to figure out what it really is. I'm excited for this whole night, really, just to be with Andrew. Especially after these past two weeks that we've spent together, I think we've solved a lot of the issues that we'd had. Not just by talking about them, but by talking about other things too. Just hanging out with each other without crazy distractions around us- just to remind each other why we ever fell in love in the first place. When he wasn't spending time with his family, he was with me and all we'd do is just talk about stuff and laugh and watch movies and hang out and it was amazing. This is the real Andrew. Not that asshole who would abandon me for video games or lie about hanging out with other girls.

"You'll understand in a minute," He tells me, parking the car before getting out to open my door for me.

"I'll understand why you brought me to a strip club?" I joke, getting out of the car and following him towards the entrance. Andrew pulls two tickets out of his wallet as we approach the door and he hands them to the bouncer, who then looks at the tickets, hands them back to Andrew, and then nods at us to continue in through the doors.

"No, you'll understand where we are and why I brought you here," He explains as we walk through a dark hallway and then through another pair of doors and just as I walk into the room, he's right. I do understand.

Inside of the huge room that we just walked into is a ginormous wall made up of glass and on the other side of that glass is water full of exotic-looking fish of various sizes. There's a lot of fancy-dressed people in the room talking amongst themselves and eating tiny finger foods from these waiters walking around the vast room and I wonder how they're not all hypnotized by this huge tank of water right there in front of them. It's there loss though, because I am completely hypnotized by all of these magical-looking fish.

"We never did go to the aquarium," I mumble, more to myself then to Andrew.

"We didn't," He agrees. "And I called ahead this time to make sure that we'd be able to get in."

"That was smart," I laugh, not taking my eyes off of the fish. I spot a clown fish and immediately think of Nemo and then I see a few large sharks and there's some sting rays too and little tiny fish and turtles swimming around. It looks like a tiny little city of coexisting little fish inside of one peaceful tank. Although I'm sure that's not the case- they probably aren't always peaceful- but it looks that way right now and I love that. They all just glide through the water beautifully as if they have no cares in the world. "This is so beautiful. I should have seen it coming."

Andrew steps up behind me and wraps his arms around my waist, pulling me close to him. "You should have. It was pretty obvious."

I roll my eyes and then turn around to face him. "Can we go eat that food over there?"

"Yes," He chuckles. "Everything's free but you can't drink the wine- they'll ID you. Other than that, it's all included in the ticket."

"I'm starving," I tell him, taking his hand in mine as we hurry over to the table that holds the large platters of food and then mini plates. There's a waiter behind the table explaining what everything is so I grab a small piece of bread topped with some type of spread that is really good.

"Everything is vegetarian," Andrew explains. "Because all of the money goes to some animal charity. It's pretty good though, right?"

"Vegetarian food can be good, you don't have to act so surprised," I chuckle at him, continuing to munch on the snack food. We already had a small dinner earlier but it was so long ago that this food tastes really good right now.

"Okay, that's true," He agrees. "Anyway, there's more than just this tank if you want to go explore."

"Was that even a question?" I ask him with a small giggle. "What are we waiting for? I want to see the manatees."

So then Andrew lets me drag him around the whole aquarium, looking at all of the different tanks that they have. Turtles, snakes, manatees, crabs, lobsters, eels, there are so many different things to look at that it's almost overwhelming. Especially when some of the rooms are empty and it'd be so romantic to kiss him right now, and I really want to so badly, and it'd be so easy since nobody else is there. It's hard to keep my hands to myself, but I just remind myself that we're taking it slow right now. After tonight, we can go crazy but tonight, we need to not rush things. Just one more night, no matter how perfect and amazing it is, we have to go slow. Luckily, though, by the time that it's 11:45, we have successfully experienced all of the tanks and we are ready for the countdown. Everybody in the aquarium moves outside to watch some fireworks that are going to go off so I start to follow them out there when Andrew pulls on my hand in the opposite direction.

"This way," He says.

"But I want to see the fireworks," I object, motioning towards the door where everybody is leaving.

"Yeah, we will. Trust me, this way is better," He assures me, tugging on my hand again.

I nod and then follow him in the wrong direction and once he has convinced me to follow him, he starts to let go of my hand, but I squeeze harder so that he knows that it's okay that we hold hands. I know that it's not a huge deal, but it's still something. His hand is large and warm and I like holding it and, although we're taking things slow, I don't think it'll kill us if we just hold hands for a little while.

"Where are we going?" I wonder when Andrew takes me to an elevator and pushes the up arrow to call the elevator to us.

"You'll see," He grins. "I think that you'll like it."

"You mean it gets better?" I ask excitedly. "Did you buy me a dolphin?"

"Unfortunately, no. I wish that I could, Stell, but I think that might be against the law. I don't know, I'll look into it," He jokes. "I'd honestly buy you the moon if I could."

"That's unnecessary. I don't want to own the moon," I assure him. "I have no idea where I'd even put the thing- it's massive. But I do appreciate the gesture."

The elevator doors slide open and we walk into the small space before Andrew pushes the top button that doesn't even read a number, it just says "RT" on the button.

"RT?" I wonder curiously. "What does that mean?"

"You're about to find out," He grins as the doors shut and then the elevator starts pulling us up to the RT level.

As we're about halfway there, it hits me and I think I understand what RT means. "Roof top?" I wonder in a voice that is probably considered a squeak.

Andrew doesn't have to answer me because by the time that I ask him, the doors are sliding open and we're walking out onto an concrete surface with the stars above us and a beautiful New Mexican cityscape to our left. Since it's the New Year, a lot of the lights are still on even at midnight and it looks so beautiful, lit up the way that it is.

"Andrew, this is beautiful," I mutter, walking over to the edge of the building. It's not a very tall building, only five stories according to the elevator buttons, so we're not that high up but high enough to see that city scape and I can see the group of party goers down on the side walk below us preparing for the fireworks at midnight to celebrate 2014. "How'd you get us up here?"

"Well, it's not against the rules, I just know about it because I used to come here a lot when I was a kid," He explains. "And I know it isn't the tallest building with the best view, I just think that it'd be nice to have a little bit of privacy for our New Year."

"Yeah, this is perfect," I agree with a nod, looking over at him with a small smile. "This whole night has been really perfect. Thank you so much."

"It's the least that I could do," He shrugs sheepishly and I see him raise his hand from his side but before it reaches me, he pauses and then drops it to his side again as if he wanted to reach out to me but then remembered that he shouldn't do that, so he decided against it.

As if to tell him that I don't mind him touching me, I step forward and wrap my arms around him in a tight hug. "You're pretty remarkable yourself, Andrew," I mutter softly into his ear.

"Not as much as you," He says quietly. "Seriously, Stella, I know that I don't deserve you. It still amazes me every day that you waste your breath on me, especially after everything that's happened."

"Because I love you," I tell him as if it's obvious, which it definitely is. That's why I stayed with him for so long through all of the video games and everything, because I love him so much and although we did break up, it was after a lot of crap. Everybody has their breaking limit and I had reached mine but he just made some mistakes and that doesn't mean that I just stopped loving him, it means that he messed up. "And just because you messed up a little doesn't mean that I'm going to stop loving you. I honestly don't think that I could even if I wanted to."

"I love you too, Stella," He tells me as we're still hugging and since we're having a moment here, I decide that I should be completely honest with him so that everything is out there. I'm used to keeping things like this to myself but just the way that he's holding me right now, I can't really help but open up to him.

"But I'm still so scared that you'll leave me again," I blurt softly into his shoulder. "I mean, there's always going to be another tournament. There's always going to be a Charlotte. You are incredibly attractive, so there's always going to be girls like that. And I know that I probably overreacted with Charlotte but that's just because I was so afraid of losing you like I've lost almost everybody else that I've ever cared about. People just get bored with me and then they leave and I was so terrified that that's what you were doing. I just started panicking and I can't guarantee that I won't do that again when it comes to girls like her. It just freaks me out."

"Stella," Andrew pulls back just far enough so that he can make eye contact with me as if to emphasize whatever point he's about to make. "It's never going to happen again, okay? Ever. I mean, sure, I'm not going to just stop playing video games but I'll admit that I got a little crazy there for a while and I know that it was ridiculous of me to do that and I'm sorry. I swear, that'll never happen again. And as for Charlotte, I was pretty naïve when it came to her. I was just trying to be her friend. I had no idea that you felt like that though. I should have listened to you more and I'm sorry. You know that I'm sorry about it."

"I know," I assure him. "You don't have to apologize anymore, it's over. I'm just trying to explain why I got so upset."

"Well, you don't have to explain yourself. Everything is in the past so let's just move on, alright? Completely fresh. Well, not completely because we obviously learned from everything that's happened but let's just put it behind us."

"Yeah," I sigh. "That sounds really good."

He pulls me closer and presses his lips to my cheek. "It's almost time for the countdown," He mumbles into my ear just as we hear the people below us beginning to countdown from ten. I think that they're listening to the radio or watching a TV so they know when to countdown, so we just follow their countdown.

3... 2... 1...

And then it's the New Year. I smile up at Andrew and then step up on my tippy toes, pressing my lips to his. He seems to be surprised by this but he only freezes for a few moments before he's kissing me back with his hand on the small of my back, bringing me close to him.

It's a really long but soft kiss and it's one of the best kisses that I've ever had in my life. I know that we had that little blip of a makeout two weeks ago, when we first got to his house, but this one is much better even though it's not as heated.

This kiss is like a promise that this year will be better. No matter what, this year will be different and this time, we will last forever.

I'm getting closer to my 1 Million votes mark and I really really wanna get there. So, I'll post the next chapter when this one gets 200 votes. Thanks so much for your help and support! You're all so fabulous <3

23 Back To School

"This is the greatest thing that has happened in all of human history," Sienna tells me on Monday as we're in the food court eating breakfast before classes.

I let out a small laugh and nod in agreement. "Yeah, it's pretty great."

"I can't believe that you two finally worked things out," Mason says. "Well, I mean, I can believe it but it's just so great. I'm definitely not going to miss all of your fighting. This is so awesome."

"Speaking of Andrew, where is he?" Sienna wonders, taking a bite of her pancake.

I shrug. "Probably with Bryan or something, I don't know."

"He's probably talking about you," Mason sings.

"Maybe," I say with a laugh. "Anyway, we went to an aquarium for New Year's Eve and then he took me up to the roof and it was pretty amazing."

"That does sound so romantic," Sienna coos and Mason eagerly nods her head in agreement. "And I want to see the bracelet. It sounds so pretty, the way that you described it over the phone."

"Oh yeah, let us see it!"

I let go of my fork and push my wrist out towards them so that they can see the gold bracelet dangling from my wrist. "His initials are engraved on the inside," I tell them. "Isn't it cute?"

"It's adorable," Sienna smiles. "He sure does know how to splurge on jewelry."

"I'm pretty sure that his mom helped him pick it out," I say, going back to eating my breakfast. After we kissed on New Year, we decided that it was the perfect time to get back together. We'd been getting along miraculously well for two full weeks and I didn't want to be without him anymore. So after that, nothing really changed between us except for the fact that we kissed. A lot. He spent a lot of time with his parents though, since they barely get to see him and once we left New Mexico, I had him all to myself.

"And I'm sure the makeup sex was amazing," Mason grins teasingly at me.

"Yeah," I nod in agreement. "I'm sure that it will be. It hasn't actually happened yet though. We only got back last night and before that, his parents were always home so it'd be weird and last night, we were both so exhausted from the flight that we just went right to bed."

"That's unacceptable," She says, shaking her head at me.

"I agree," I say with a laugh, noticing Sienna look down at her phone and then her face noticeably drops. "Something wrong?" I ask her.

She looks up at me and then shrugs. "No. It's just Penn's sister. Ana, they're having issues with her again."

I remember Ana from a while ago, she's Penn's little sister, only a year younger than us. I don't know too much about her story but I know that she was depressed and suicidal so her parents sent her away to Alaska or something but she came back home over the summer but I guess she isn't completely better- I don't even know if there is a 'completely better' in this situation.

"What's wrong with her?" Mason asks.

"I don't know, I'm going over to Penn's tonight to see," Sienna tells us. "He's really worried about her."

"I'm sure everything will be fine," Mason tells her with an assuring smile. "Let us know if there's anything we can do to help out or anything."

"Yeah, thanks. I'll do that. Right now though, we have to get to class."

Mason checks the time on her phone and then nods before we all stand up and throw away our now-empty trays and then make our way towards the academic building for first period. Everybody is so mopey today because it's the first day back from winter break, but I'm in such a good mood because of my fixed relationship with Andrew so it's kind of weird to be the only chirpy one walking down the hallway but I'll get over it.

I'm walking with Sienna towards our calculus class when we're bombarded by a tall person jumping in front of us. Andrew grins down at me and I hear Sienna giggle beside me.

"Why aren't you in class?" I ask him with raised eyebrows.

"Because I don't feel like doing to class," He tells me with a shrug. "Come on, let's go do something. Everybody here is so depressing with their bad moods and everything."

"We have class though," I remind him with a small giggle that escapes my lips.

"Oh, come on, Stell, you can skip just for today," Sienna chimes with a wide grin as she starts walking away, into the math wing of the building. "I'll see you guys later."

I wave to her before turning my attention back to Andrew and then we side step so that we're not in the way of anybody that's walking through the hallways. "Where would we go if I agreed to skip with you?"

He shrugs. "I don't know. We could go get ice cream or something. Whatever you want to do."

"Ice cream does sound good," I decide with a long sigh. "You're being a bad influence on me, you know."

Andrew takes my hand in his and then leads me out of the math wing towards the front doors of the building. "Yeah, I think I can live with myself. I mean, it is only one day and we can come back for dance practice."

"It's still bad though," I tell him.

We walk out of the academic building and make it all the way into the field behind the building before the first bell rings. We can't go through campus because there's a security guard that walks around to make sure that nobody is skipping. Fortunately, though, they haven't caught on to the fact that people just cut through the fields and get out that way pretty easily. It's such a nice day outside that instead of going for ice cream, we decide to just sit in the field behind the rec center under a shady tree. I'm wearing capris so the grass only manages to feel scratchy on my ankles.

"So how has your day been?" Andrew asks me as we're sitting in the grass, facing away from the bright morning sun.

"It's only eight in the morning," I remind him. "The only thing that I've done so far is wake up and eat breakfast. What about you?"

He shrugs. "It's been okay. I got you something though."

"You did?" I repeat. "We've only been apart for less than twelve hours, what could you have possibly gotten me in that time period?"

He grins at me and then pulls a colorful bunch of flowers out of his school bag. "It was really hard for me not to smash them in there but I managed pretty well, I think. Do you like them?"

I take the fresh flowers from his hand and then examine all of the beautiful colors- yellows, reds, purples, pinks, blues. "It's gorgeous," I tell him with a small smile before leaning over and pressing my lips to his. "Thanks, Andrew. I miss getting flowers."

"I know, that's why I got them for you," He smiles at me. "I was trying to be spontaneous."

"Well, it is very spontaneous," I chuckle. "Skipping school and flowers- it all just screams romance."

"Doesn't it?" He jokes. "I'm basically Romeo."

"Romeo and Juliet died though," I remind him. "I don't want to be like them."

"I didn't mean exactly like them," He laughs. "Just a little bit."

"Okay then," I chuckle, leaning into his side causing him to reflexively wrap his arm around my waist. "Sienna and Mason really like the bracelet that you got me."

"Oh, that's good. I really only got it for them," Andrew says jokingly.

"They wish," I scoff but I'm obviously just kidding because that'd be really weird if Andrew bought me a bracelet just to impress my friends. "Have you talked to Charlotte yet?"

I can feel him tense up beside me as I change the subject to something thornier for us. "No, I haven't. Why?"

I shrug. "Just curious. I think she'll try to make a scene in rehearsal today when she finds out that we're back together. She doesn't seem like the kind of girl that's used to losing."

"I'm sure she'll get over it," Andrew tells me. "And if not, then it's not really our problem."

"Since when don't you like her anyway? You used to want to be her best buddy but you never told me what changed your mind," I wonder.

"Okay, right before the Christmas show, she tried to turn me completely against you and then when I told her that you weren't a bad person and that I still loved you, she had a fit and it was just obvious that she wasn't as nice as I thought that she was," He explains to me.

"I told you that my psycho girl instincts are spot on," I sing. "Like with Gianna- I immediately knew that she was an incredible bitch but nobody believed me until she started dating Anthony."

"Well, I know now so that's all that matters, right?"

"Yeah," I agree with him. "That's all that matters."

"You don't have to worry about Charlotte," He assures me.

"I know," I sigh, leaning farther into him. "I trust you and everything, I just really hate that girl. I'm tired of dealing with her."

"Let's just not talk about it," Andrew suggests. "She's not going away so it's just going to make it worse by talking about her even more."

"You're right," I sigh. "Let's talk about how we should go out to dinner tonight."

"Dinner?" He echoes. "Why do you want to go to dinner?"

"I feel like it'll make tonight more special if we go out to dinner first," I explain, moving so that I'm laying down and my head is resting on his lap.

"Wait, what's happening tonight?" Andrew wonders, obviously a little confused, seeming to feel a little bit panicked that he forgot something that was supposed to happen tonight.

"Well, I just figured that we're back together and everything and we'll finally have some time to ourselves, so I just figured that we'd make the night… special," I explain to him with a shy smile playing at the corners of my mouth.

"And by special, you mean…?" He trails off and I can see that he's leaning over, his face getting closer to mine.

I sit up and grin at him. "I mean that we should go out to dinner."

He presses his lips to mine for a quick kiss. "Just dinner then?"

"Of course," I joke coyly. "I don't know what else we could possibly do."

He doesn't even justify my remark with a response, he just presses his lips to mine again and then rolls us over in the grass, causing me to giggle and then respond to his kiss.

We lay in the grass like that for a while just making out, and it gets pretty heated, but we don't go too far because I'm too paranoid that somebody would find us and that'd be really, extremely awkward.

So we make out and talk for a little longer before we decide to actually get out of the grass and walk over to get ice cream just before it's time to make it back to campus for dance rehearsal, since it'd be really stupid to skip dance because we'd miss a lot more than just some notes like in a regular class room.

I give Andrew a quick kiss once we get into the dance studio for class and then head into the back where the girls' locker room is but just as I get to my locker, somebody steps in front of me.

I let out a soft groan when I recognize Charlotte's obnoxious frown in front of me. "Stella," She says my name as some sort of greeting, crosses her arms over her chest, and then continues. "How was your break?"

I toss my gym bag onto the bench in front of my locker and then start opening it. "Oh, it was fantastic, thanks for asking."

"I saw you with Andrew out there," She tells me as if she has caught me in some huge lie or something.

"Did you? That's really surprising considering we walked in together holding hands in front of everyone. Super shocking," I mutter sarcastically, hoping that she gets the memo that I don't want to talk to her right now. Or ever. "Did you like the show?"

"You're repulsive," She sneers at me as I slip my shoes off of my feet so that I can get dressed in my workout clothes.

"Yeah, okay then," I amuse her. "That's nice. Good to know."

"Hey, I don't know you think that you are, but-"

I slide my pink "New York" shirt over my head to exchange it for my razor back tank top as I interrupt her would-be rant. "I think that I'm Stella Wayne. And I think that you're Charlotte Whatever-the-fuck-your-last-name-is. I also think that you need to stay the hell away from me. And preferably Andrew too but if you want to talk to him then you go ahead but he'll turn you down faster than Kim Kardashian's last marriage. I know that you think that you're hot shit but you've only got half of that right. And I think we both know that it's definitely not the hot part."

Her eyes widen, surprised at my long outburst as I start to change into my yoga shorts. She opens her mouth to say something else, but I'm not having any of it.

"I'm done talking to you now," I tell her, sliding my shorts up and then throwing my hair into a pony tail, paying no attention to her but she just stays there. She doesn't say anything, she looks like she's still dumfounded by what I said and I don't know why because I don't think what I said was too harsh or mean or anything. "This is the part where you walk away," I remind her slowly.

She blinks at me a few times but then finally listens to me and turns and walks away without another snide comment, which was a major relief.

I put my shoes on, put all of my stuff in my locker, and then leave the room, putting everything behind me for good.

24 Epilogues

Seven Years Later

"This is Broadway, people!" Cenzia yells at all of us as we're basically heaving for breath in our rehearsal studio. "We're going one more time before rehearsal is over."

I share an exhausted look with one of my co-dancers, Brie, as everybody walks back to their starting position to start the show over again just so that we can do it right and then go home. Not that I don't love practice, but we've been working on this scene for four hours straight now and it's getting around dinner time, which means that I'm hungry and I have dinner plans with Andrew.

This is my third Broadway show and this time, I'm actually the lead actress, which is amazing. Especially considering this has been my dream for years- since I was little, actually. Not just being on Broadway but being the lead in a Broadway play. It kind of proves to everyone who ever doubted me that I could make it. Almost my whole family, Gianna and Charlotte and everybody like that. It proves it to myself that I can do it.

Cenzia, one of our lead choreographers, starts the music again and then we count down like we always do and then start the dance. I have to sing too, since I'm the lead, but we're not adding the vocals with the dancing yet. After getting my first Broadway gig right after I graduated Julliard, I realized that I'd get better roles if I took up singing too, so that's what I did. I took extensive singing lessons until I was able to get a minor singing role in another play and then, I finally was able to audition for the role and after a few auditions, I got this lead. I know that I'm not the best singer ever but I'm pretty good, I think, and my dancing makes up for not being the best.

Anyway, we finish the scene and then Cenzia releases us for the day just so that she can go pull some more of her own hair out. Cenzia is really nice and everything but it's a week before opening weekend so she's extremely stressed out right now, so we all understand her snappiness and everything.

"So, are you getting nervous?" Brie asks me in the busy locker room as I toss my gym bag over my shoulder and we start to leave the locker room.

"I've been nervous since I got the call that I got the role," I chuckle. "I feel like I'm going to vomit."

"Please," She scoffs. "You were born to play this part. Literally, you've been training for this your whole life. You have nothing to worry about."

"Let's hope so," I sigh. "Are you nervous at all?"

"Me? I'm just backup," She reminds me.

"That doesn't mean that you can't be nervous. When I was backup, I was nervous," I assure her. "My boyfriend said that he thought that I was going to go bald before the show- which of course didn't make things any better."

"Boyfriend?" Brie repeats with a frown. "I thought that you're married."

"Well, I am, but he was my boyfriend at the time," I explain, referring to Andrew, who I hadn't married until I was twenty-four, last year, and my first Broadway show was when I was twenty. "But anyway, Broadway is always crazy- it's always nerve racking."

"Speaking of boyfriend-slash-husband," Brie grins as we stop just outside the door of our rehearsal building when we both see Andrew standing there on the sidewalk waiting for me, I assume.

I smile and wave at him before turning to Brie. "I'll see you tomorrow."

"Yeah, see you tomorrow," She laughs before we part ways and I hurry over to my beautiful husband.

"Hey," I chirp, wrapping my arms around him and placing a soft kiss on his lips.

"Hey," He kisses me back.

"What are you doing here? I thought we were meeting at home to go to dinner," I tell him as he voluntarily takes my gym bag from my shoulder because he's such a gentleman and insists on carrying it for me on our way home.

"We were," He assures me, chewing nervously on his bottom lip. He doesn't start walking down the sidewalk like I expected him to, he just stands there and I start to suspect that something is wrong.

"What's up?" I wonder with a small frown.

"Well, I got home from work today and I found something in the apartment. Now, I remember that you said that we should go out to dinner because you had something to tell me and I was going to wait until you got home but I couldn't wait. So, I found this and I was wondering if the news that you have to tell me at dinner has anything to do with this?" He rambles until he pulls out a little plastic bag with a thin white stick inside and on the end of that stick, there's a little pink plus sign.

I'd taken that pregnancy test this morning and tossed it in the trashcan in our bathroom but I didn't think that Andrew would find it. I take a deep breath and look up at him. "I didn't want to tell you until I was sure. And I wanted it to be special," I say, feeling myself get choked up for almost no reason at all.

"And how sure are you now?" He asks me, a smile poking at the corners of his mouth, trying his hardest to contain his excitement.

With a small laugh, I tell him, "I've taken three different tests and they all say the same thing."

"Oh my god," He grins at me before lunging forward and lifting me into the air, spinning me around in circles as I erupt in light giggles. "Oh my god," He says again and then he kisses me. "We're going to have a baby?"

"I think so. I need to schedule an appointment tonight but I wanted to tell you first," I explain.

"This is so cool," He tells me, putting me down again and resting his hand on my belly, although it's still flat (and very sweaty). "This is amazing. Wait... but what about your show?"

"I actually already have it figured out. I'll probably be able to finish this show and then after that, I can get an instructor position until I can start dancing again. I'll have to talk all of that through with the doctor though. We'll figure it out," I assure him with a small smile. "I'm really glad that you're happy about this."

"Of course I am," Andrew assures me. "Why wouldn't I be? We're going to have our own little nugget of humanness. That is so cool."

I hold his hand in mine as we start on our journey home and since we live in the heart of New York City, we just take the subway everywhere instead of driving and the closest subway station is only a few blocks away. "I don't know. We just never really talked about kids or anything," I explain to him with a small shrug.

"Well, I think that we'll be awesome parents. I can teach him how to play baseball in the front yard and teach him about girls and everything," He tells me.

"He?" I echo. "What if she's a girl though?"

"Then I'll teach her how to stay away from boys for her entire life," He says. "And we'll probably go bankrupt with all of the clothes that you'll buy her. What if we have twins? We should get a dog."

"A dog?"

He shrugs. "I don't know, I'm just so excited right now, I don't know what to think. How are we going to tell everybody? They'll be so excited too."

"Well, I was thinking that almost everybody is coming to my opening show so we can make the announcement at the after party. Even Anthony said that he's coming from Texas."

"He's still there?"

I nod. My brother decided to go to Texas for college and he just decided to stay there because he loved it so much. As a result, I haven't seen him since we graduated high school, even for holidays and everything, he just stays there in Texas. Since high school, we never were close so it's not like a major loss for me and we still email sometimes, but I am kind of excited to see him now since it's been so long. I'm not sure exactly what he does there in Texas, I just know that he really loves it and I think he has a girlfriend or something. "I don't think my parents are coming but that's whatever. They were always so ashamed of me going to Broadway."

"Yeah," He sighs. "I don't care what our kid wants to do- they can do it. Unless they want to become a drug dealer or something. But other than that, I'll be proud no matter what."

"Me too," I lean into his side and he wraps his arm around my shoulders. "But Sienna and Penn are flying in from Seattle. Mason and Bryan are getting a babysitter for Wyatt and Emma and they're coming too."

Sienna had moved to Seattle with her boyfriend, Penn, after college and then a few years later, they got married but they're still holding off with starting a family because Sienna is still building her career as a dance teacher for little kids so she wants to wait. As for Brian and Mason, they already have two. After graduating from Berkeley, they moved back to LA to be close to their families. Mason got a major in tourism and event planning so she's going to be a wedding planner, hopefully, she'll start her own business after a while. At least, that's what she wants to do. Brian got a major in computer science so he's got a job for some program software company.

A few years ago, they had Wyatt and then just a few months ago, Emma was born, which is amazing for them. I think Mason wants a big family so they have an amazing start for now. Luckily, though, they have awesome parents who love their grandchildren and will allow Mason and Brian to travel to New York for a few days to watch my debut show. Being the lead and everything, this is kind of a huge deal so almost everybody that's important to me is trying to make it. Even Andrew's parents and his brother, Lucas, are coming.

"I have no idea how to change a diaper," Andrew tells me. "Or how to breast feed."

"I think that second one is my job, babe," I laugh, kissing his cheek as we continue walking down the sidewalk. "But as for changing a diaper, you should definitely learn because I'm not doing all of that on my own. You have plenty of time though, these things take a whole nine months to bake, you know."

"Yeah, but there's so much other stuff to do too," He says. "We have to build a nursery. We have that guest bedroom that we barely ever use, so we can use that."

"Andrew, you're going to be the best dad ever," I assure him. "I promise. Our baby is going to be the most awesome little human nugget that has ever existed."

"She might take over the world," He suggests.

I laugh a little bit. "I wouldn't put it past her. We better stay on her good side."

Andrew takes his arm away from my waist and then holds my left hand in his right one, his thumb running along the diamond ring that lays on my ring finger. "I love you so much, you know."

"I love you so much too," I tell him. "That's kind of why I married you."

"Really?" He wonders sarcastically. "I thought it was just for my astonishing good looks."

"Well, that too. Mostly that, actually," I joke. "But a little bit because I love you."

"I can live with that," He smiles, kissing my temple. "But anyway, seriously, do you want a boy or a girl?"

I shrug. "I don't care. I'll love him or her either way. He or she will be fabulous no matter what, we'll make sure of that."

"Of course," He agrees with a nod. "And totally awesome and kick-ass."

"But you can't say kick-ass around a baby. You'll have to watch your language," I warn him. "No cursing at all."

"Right," He nods, rubbing my tummy again. "Sorry, little nugget."

I can't help but laugh at that. "And when you call her a nugget, you kind of sound like you want to eat her."

"No I don't," He argues. "There's not just chicken nuggets, you know. There's gold nuggets too. He or she is more like gold than chicken, I think."

"Definitely gold," I grin. "This is going to be so much fun."

"The pregnancy?" Andrew wonders.

"God, no," I scoff, wincing now just thinking about all of the pain that Mason went through with both of her pregnancies. I know that it'll be worth it but it still won't be fun at all. "I just mean like, the rest of our lives... with our little gold nugget of human and with each other and New York and my dancing and your doctoring. We're set for life now."

Back in high school, I can't believe I was so caught up with the "cupcake phase" of a relationship. That's not real, that's just acute infatuation and that's okay for the beginning of a relationship but it isn't real. It isn't love. This- what I have with Andrew now- this is love. We fight sometimes but we work it out. We get annoyed by each other sometimes. We don't spend every second of every day together. It might not sound as glamorous as the beginning but it's so much better. It's harder, I'll admit that, but it's worth it. It's the difference between thinking somebody is completely perfect and realizing that they aren't perfect but loving them anyway.

"You're right," He agrees, kissing my lips and then pulling me close to his side. "This is going to be so much fun."

THE END

www.ingramcontent.com/pod-product-compliance
Lightning Source LLC
Chambersburg PA
CBHW072150070526
44585CB00015B/1083